Your Comfort Zone is Killing You

Billy Anderson
founder, the courage crusade

Cover illustration and design: The Tite Group
Author photo by Bellatrix Photography

This book is dedicated to you

"It takes courage to grow up and turn out
to be who you really are."

E. E. Cummings

The adventure continues, my good man!

Billy

Table of Stuff

PART 1 - WARM-UP

My Promise To You

This book will help ensure that at the end of your life, you don't share the #1 regret of people on their deathbed:

"I wish I'd had the courage to live a life true to myself, not the life others expected of me."

I'll take you through a *process* that uncovers the courageous person you're meant to be, allowing you to love who you are, live true to yourself and feel strong enough to carve your own path in life. Your authenticity will be an inspiration to people all around you.

And damn you'll have fun.

This book is based on REAL LIFE experiences of myself and my clients, not on research done to rats or focus groups desperately trying to prove an already-determined point. I will lay it all on the table so you can learn from our victories, our screw-ups and our embarrassing moments.

These real-life stories will appear throughout the book and they further explain the theories being discussed. Let's start with one right now about one of the scariest changes I made in my life that would allow the real me to come out...

Story Time

I was terrified. I felt alone. Was this a stupid decision? It was day one of my new life and I was sitting in a canoe.

I had just quit my advertising career that I had started in Europe and continued in Canada. It was the career I spent 4 years at university preparing for. I quit because my life wasn't as fulfilling as I wanted and expected it would be. It didn't allow me to be me.

So now I was following my dreams: leading wilderness trips with Outward Bound Canada.

But how could this be a "job"? Instead of sitting at a desk I was sitting in a canoe. Instead of a keyboard and mouse in my hand I had a screwdriver (I was fixing the seat, which I wasn't totally sure how to do). How could this be a *career*?! Were my city friends right - was I nuts to leave a well-paying corporate job to do THIS?!

My mind was flooded with uncertainty. "Oh crap, is this what I really want?" "What if this doesn't work?" "Am I too old to make this kind of change?" "Why didn't I just keep playing it safe?" "Do people think I'm stupid for doing this?" *"What if I fail?!"*

Read on, and get ready to live the kind of life that makes you jump out of bed and dance to the radio.

I'm proud of you already ☺

What might you take away from this book?

- Having more confidence in your decisions.
- Comparing yourself less to other people.
- Gaining comfort with failure.
- Asking for (and getting) what you want.
- Caring less what other people think of you.
- Sticking up for what you believe in.
- Managing your emotions so they don't get you in deep water.
- Not shying away from scary conversations in your personal life or at work.

This can lead to...

- Feeling extremely proud of who you are.
- Getting more clear on what life/career path is right for you.
- Surrounding yourself with the right people.
- Improving or ending bad relationships.
- Starting your own business.
- Asking for a raise or promotion.
- Finding the kind of partner you actually deserve, rather than feeling like you're "settling" for someone.
- Leaving a job in order to get the kind of career you've always wanted but didn't have the guts to go for.

My Story of Struggle

"Where there is no struggle, there is no strength."
Oprah Winfrey

I was 5 years old. My mom heard me crying in my room so she came in to see what was wrong. Through my tears I said, "You're born, you live for a while, then you die. What's the point?"

The rest of my life has been dedicated to figuring out that "point" and how to make it a reality. Through my journey of experimentation, world travel and countless adventures - some good, some bad - I discovered the importance of courage as a means to figuring out who I was and carving my own amazing path while caring less about being judged by others. But it's been a scary, bumpy road.

I struggled through a deep depression at the age of 15; deep enough that I had a psychiatrist, group therapy, and anti-depression medication. I wasn't doing as well in school and for the first time in my life I didn't feel like the perfect son. I felt like I was letting down my parents - the two people I wanted most to be proud of me. They never gave any indication whatsoever that I let them down, they were still just as loving and supportive as they'd always been. But I felt worthless. On top of this, I was no longer one of the "cool" kids at school. A few kids were making fun of me which had never happened before. I felt lost. I even contemplated suicide.

In hopes of finding a place that was a better fit, I left that all-boys private school and struggled to fit into my local high school. A school that had girls! (Read: terrifying) A school without a dress code where I had to pretend to know what was in style then feel confident wearing it.

As an adult I struggled to make sense of a terrible car accident I was in that left a man dead.

During my travels in poor countries I struggled to understand why people who had so little could be so much happier than most of us in North America where we seem to have everything. I felt guilty for what I had. Why was I so lucky to be born in Canada with an amazingly supportive family?

I struggled to figure out the career path that was best for me. I found myself in a career that I didn't enjoy, even though it paid well, was respected and was what society said was the kind of career and life I *should* be having. But I didn't like it! I wanted a career that would bring out my inner superhero, help me make a positive difference in the world and *not* make me depressed when I got out of bed every Monday morning.

Whether you have gone through similar struggles or you've had completely different ones, we all struggle through life. But unfortunately, many people don't openly discuss their struggles with others and, as a result, very often never figure out how best to get through them! This book shows you how to figure that out and become the person you're meant to be.

My Story of Success

"I know where I'm going and I know the truth,
and I don't have to be what you want me to be.
I'm free to be what I want."
Muhammad Ali

I've spent my entire life figuring "it" out: facing my fears, not accepting mediocrity, continually pushing myself to be better, seeking out what I truly wanted and how I was going to be amazing at it. I now march to the beat of my own drum and I do not let society's expectations dictate my path. I don't settle. If I don't like something I accept it or I change it as quickly as possible.

I'm also very aware; aware that I'm not perfect and I never will be, but I am 100% in control of my life. I am confident in what I'm doing and where I'm going.

Years ago I left that comfortable, well-paying, respected career in order to pursue my dreams. I went from working at a desk in the corporate world to leading canoe trips in the wilderness and being a freelance writer. It was terrifying. I doubted myself every step of the way. I kept imagining what people would say if it didn't work out: "See, I told you it was crazy."

I had the guts to change careers two *more* times on my search for the one that was perfect for me. I then started my own business. I now love what I do so much that I no longer say "I run a Coaching and Speaking business" because it just doesn't feel like work. Now I say "I help people find the courage to be themself. And sometimes I get paid for it."

I found the girl of my dreams, overcame my own negative stereotypes of marriage and "settling down", and now she's my ridiculously amazing wife. This took a ton of self-

---

12

reflection, of digging into my own limiting beliefs, of being honest with myself about who I really was and what I was afraid of.

I know what I'm amazing at, I know how I can make a difference, and I live true to it every day. I don't compare myself to others anymore. The only person I compare myself to is the person I was yesterday. This provides me with a level of self-confidence I never had before. That feels GOOD.

I have now surrounded myself with friends and colleagues who support me and what I want in my life. They challenge me to be better. I've ditched the people who don't.

I am now a professionally licensed Coach, a keynote speaker, a certified Career Consultant, and a regular contributor to Canada's national newspaper, The Globe and Mail.

And I'm happy. Holy smokes am I ever happy! When we are being 100% authentic we attract the right opportunities and the right people that provide us with *fulfillment* (happiness on steroids).

One of the proudest accomplishments of my entire life was when I walked 200 kms in the middle of winter to raise money for kids with cancer. I also carried a canoe 42 kms in two days to send needy kids to summer camp. I still feel all warm and cuddly inside thinking about the positive impact those efforts had on kids.

I entered a story-telling competition with a children's book that I wrote, even though I was nervous someone might say, "You wrote a book about a duck? Why?" I won first place!

I did stand-up comedy in front of a crowd of strangers. My hands were shaking the whole time but it was so empowering not to back down from the fear of failure.

I have also pushed myself to understand my physical limits and reaction to danger. I have jumped out of an airplane exactly 101 times. I have traveled to over 30 countries. I have bungee-jumped on two different continents, gone hang-gliding in the French Alps and swam with sharks in Asia and South America. I ran with the bulls in Spain and I got trampled. I have a scar to prove it!

Throughout this journey I have always considered other people's advice and opinions, but I make my own decisions based on how well I know myself and what my goals are. Damn that's exciting.

I'm definitely not perfect but I am trying to be the best I can be, every damn day. I know that if I die tomorrow the world is a better place because I was here.

Because I've been on this winding, crazy road of experience and I'm sharing it with you in this book, you can save yourself so much time, hassle and confusion. Get ready to absorb a lifetime of hands-on learning so you can skip the crap and go straight to filling the amazing shoes that you alone were meant to fill.

Your Present Situation

Before you continue on this life-changing adventure, let's take a look at your present situation and identify the areas in your life that you are not totally satisfied with right now. You can choose any areas which you would like to improve or be different, but don't think about it too much. Write down what comes to mind and make it as long as you like - no one will see it but you! Grab a pen and paper and make a list now.

Did you make your list? If not, stop reading, go back and do your list! It'll help immensely.

The parts of your life which you're not happy or satisfied with are often the parts where you're probably not being true to yourself. Another word for this is "fit". Everything feels better when it fits, from a sexy pair of undies to the perfect career. If your job is well-matched with your skills and your purpose, it *fits*. If your spouse has similar values to yours, makes you laugh and supports you, that's a great *fit*. Conversely, if you argue with your family all the time then how you treat each other doesn't fit your wants and needs (nor theirs probably).

If you're not happy in your job or career, there's a good chance it either doesn't allow you to use your skills - whether or not you actually know what those skills are - or you don't align with the purpose of the organization or the culture (whether you know your own purpose or not). If you get fired by your company it's not because you're no good, it's simply a matter of poor fit.

Put up your hand if you've ever been dumped by a significant other. You can't see me but my hand is up. That simply means the fit wasn't there, and the other person saw it before you did. Sometimes we both see the poor fit, but the other person simply acts on it first because we're so scared of being alone that we avoid initiating the conversation.

Identifying the poor fits in your life gives you something to aim at. All the tips, tricks and processes in this book will be way more valuable if you apply them to real-life situations.

Now that you know this, is there anything else you would add or change about your list? If you felt stuck making your unhappy list, here are a few common things my clients are not satisfied with when they first come to me:

Career

- "I dread getting up for work every day."
- "I feel lost in my job. I don't feel like I'm making a difference."
- "I avoid difficult conversations."
- "I don't think my boss or team appreciates me. They don't recognize my input."
- "I want to quit, but what would I do? What if I can't find anything?"
- "I want to go back to school, but how do I make this happen? And what should I study?"

Personal

- "I don't know what I'm good at."
- "I question my decisions."
- "I don't feel supported."
- "I'm scared to be honest about what I really think, so I keep it to myself."
- "I'm tired of not feeling valued."
- "My family doesn't listen to what I really want, they just hear what THEY want."
- "My emotions get the best of me sometimes."
- "I feel like I'm constantly putting the needs of others before my own."

Romance

- "I'm lonely. I can't summon the courage to talk to THAT person I keep thinking about."
- "I sometimes say hurtful things to my spouse."
- "I feel like I'm compromising too much in my relationship."
- "I don't feel respected."
- "Is this person 'the one'?"

Why is it so hard to live true to yourself?

Let's go back to the #1 deathbed regret...

"I wish I'd had the courage to live a life true to myself, not the life others expected of me."

It's easy to see the benefits of "living a life that's true to myself" and not allowing others to dictate it for you. But do you see the word "courage" in there? Why is that needed? Couldn't it just say "I wish I'd lived a life true to myself, not the life others expected of me"? What significance does courage play in making all this true-to-myself stuff happen?

Take a look at the 4 areas in the graph below. Have you ever said any of those things? Do they relate to any of the items in your list?

Every change or improvement that you would like to make fits into one of the quadrants. Sometimes it's more obvious than others. If you love your career and you know where you want to go with it, you're probably in the top right quadrant because you're very "clear" and you're "taking action". That's a good place to be! Or perhaps you know what job or career might make you happier but you don't know how to make it happen. You're in the top left quadrant. Perhaps your romantic relationship (we'll refer to that person as your "one-and-only" from now on, since that is what I call my wife) is a real pain in the you-know-what and a complete drain on your life and you're feeling like the relationship might need to come to an end. But you can't decide. You're in the bottom left quadrant.

Sometimes it's not obvious which quadrant applies because what you're unhappy with seems to depend on other people or things. In that case, you want to focus on "What part of this is within my control?" If you're not happy with how someone is treating you, it's in your control to stick up for yourself, explain your frustration to that person (nicely) and how you would prefer they treated you. You first have to get clear on why you're unhappy about it, then take action to explain it to them and help reach a compromise.

We want to get to the top right quadrant where we know what we want and we are confident in our plan to get it.

Exercise

Look back at your Unhappy List. Place each of those things in the appropriate boxes of the graph. If you're stuck with one, ask yourself "What control do I have over this?"

Now what do we do?

While taking action is important, the first step is always to get clear (the vertical axis in the diagram). Another term for this, which we tend to hear a lot about, is "self-awareness". But I prefer the word clear - it sounds a little less Freudian and a bit more like everyday language.

The first half of this book is about getting clear.

We want to get clear on what's important to us, what we're good at, what we want to achieve with our life and what fears are presently holding us back from getting it. And believe me, fear is holding ALL of us back, myself included. Fear doesn't feel good! That's why most people avoid getting clear... because it's scary. We need courage to face scary questions like, "What if I never figure this out?" "What if other people don't like the real me?" "What if I realize I'm not good at anything?" "What if I want something that is different than other people - what will they think of me?" "What if I can't have what I want?" It takes bucket-loads of courage to face these fears.

There's an even bigger reason why getting clear is scary: we may realize that our present situation isn't right for us, meaning we'll have to CHANGE something. Change requires courage because every part of our DNA is screaming at us not to change anything. It's programmed into us. The next chapter will explain why.

Once we tell our fears to scram and we get clear on what we need to do to move forward, we then have to start *doing* things to bring it all to life: Taking Action (the horizontal axis of the diagram). That's the second half of this book.

Taking action is scary for a whole bunch of reasons. "Will people judge me? What if I fail?" Failing *sucks* (join the club, I hate it too). It is so much easier just to keep doing what you've been doing because it's *familiar*. It's safe. But imagine it's 5 years from now and your life is exactly the same. Those unsatisfied areas in your life which you listed earlier haven't improved. How would *that* feel?

Sometimes I meet people who THINK they're clear. They think they know what they want and they have a plan to get it.

But when I ask them a few questions to get them thinking about it a bit deeper, they often discover there may be a few stones unturned, or they realize they had beliefs or fears that were getting in the way of the real them coming out. This is very, very common.

I made a big mistake when I started writing this book. I didn't spend NEARLY enough time getting clear on exactly what I wanted to deliver and how it would have to be structured in order to make that happen. I was so excited to write (Taking Action) that I just dove into the writing without a proper plan. It meant that I had to go back and spend a ton of time re-organizing (Getting Clear). I wish I had done that at the beginning! The writing process would have been much quicker and WAY less frustrating. I wouldn't have felt like a mouse in a maze with no clue how to get to the cheese.

Story Time

I was once giving a keynote speech to an audience of 600 people. A lady in the front row put up her hand and said, "But I don't think I need any more courage." I replied, "You're absolutely right, you don't need more courage. If you're not starving and your life isn't in danger then nature is happy with you because you're surviving. But the more important question is: do you *want* more courage?"

The look on her face changed from an "I'm right and I know everything" to "Aw shucks, yeah, I wouldn't mind a bit more courage." Her physical state changed instantly. She relaxed, lost the look of defiance and smiled innocently like a little kid. Kids are honest. They say what they feel. She was allowing herself to let her guard down, let the real her come through, and admit that maybe she could get even MORE out of her life than she already was.

Let's be clear - you don't NEED more courage. You're living

and breathing - that's all nature cares about. But without courage, that list you made isn't going to change. And I want you to be happier and more fulfilled than a pig in poop.

One more thing...

In order for the most authentic, amazing you to bound out your door every day, you need to feel like you're worth it. Like you deserve to be happier and more fulfilled than you currently feel. If you don't already believe that you truly deserve this, you will struggle more with gaining the courage to build a life that fits you as an individual. You'll second-guess yourself and you'll assume that other people know better. If this sounds like you, don't worry, you're not alone. In fact, I find a huge percentage of people feel this way, including me earlier in my life. I have had many, many clients realize they didn't feel that they mattered enough, that they didn't add any value, that people didn't respect them, that their opinion didn't really count.

Or sometimes they feel like they're happy *enough* - "Who am I to ask for more than I've already got? I have more than a lot of people have, shouldn't I be satisfied with that? Will people think I'm too selfish?"

Take a moment right now to look in the mirror and say to yourself, "I deserve to be even happier and to love my life more." Find a mirror and say that now. No mirror? Then just say it out loud (but a mirror works way better, so try it later).

How did it feel? Did it come easily or did it make you uncomfortable?

That's why we start with getting clear. Once you know what you're good at (and believe me, you are extremely good at something), and once you discover what's important to you,

you can see that you matter and you deserve more because you will discover how you can have an *impact*. Being the amazing you that you're meant to be comes from being PROUD of the person you choose to be every day. If you're not really proud of who you are, you will have a very hard time accepting that other people actually like you and value you.

So if you need to, repeat this every day and you will slowly start to believe it: "I deserve to be as happy as a pig in poop. I have what it takes to live with courage. I am uniquely awesome and I want to be 100% me."

If you already know you matter and you are confident you have the right to ask for more fulfillment in life, awesome! This book will show you how to get it quicker and more consistently. If you don't have a CLUE about any of this and it all seems impossible, don't worry. It will be laid out for you clearly.

I get shivers just writing about this stuff! I am so damn excited to have you here and to help you rock your life even more than you already are. I consider myself the luckiest guy in the world to be your partner in this journey.

Giddy up.

PART 2 - GETTING CLEAR

ON COURAGE

Courage is Hard

Did you notice in the previous section that the word 'courage' often shows up in the same sentence as the words 'fear' or 'scary'?

Story Time

A 28-year old man is celebrating New Year's Eve with his brother on vacation. At 3am they're driving back to their campsite. Up ahead on the side of the road, a man is arguing with his fiancée. At the last second, the man tries to cross the highway in front of the car. The driver is unable to stop in time. The man is hit head-on and dies.

After the police clear the driver who was not under the influence of alcohol and was therefore not at fault, he flies home the next day. He sits on his couch alone, playing back the events of the previous night in his head. He sits there for hours until it gets dark outside. Then he gets in his car and goes driving on the highway, knowing that if he doesn't get back on that horse right away, he might never do it again.

The driver of that car was me. I still have a perfectly clear picture of the man's face hitting the windshield directly in front of me. I remember the awful sound it made, the feeling of the windshield collapsing in on me, and the image of him rolling off the car as I skidded to a halt. I can still see him lying there on the pavement.

That night after the accident, when I was back home driving on the highway, I cried the entire time. I was terrified as I drove that it might happen again, that I might hear that same horrible sound and realize that a man was dead. It was one of the hardest things I've ever done, getting back in that car and being on the highway. But this is true for all courageous acts - they are difficult because fear is involved.

The worst definition of courage I have ever seen is this: "The quality of mind or spirit that enables a person to face difficulty, danger, pain, etc., without fear."

Tsk tsk. It's this kind of thinking that makes people underestimate the courage they already have and stops them from becoming *more* courageous. Courage can NOT exist without fear. If you're not scared while you do something, you're not being courageous. I consider myself to be one of the most courageous people I've ever met, which simply means I'm scared more often than most people are. In fact, I'm scared all the time because I choose to be courageous rather than choose to be cowed by fear.

Here's a great definition of courage:
- "Mental or moral strength to venture, persevere, and *withstand* danger, fear, or difficulty."

Steve Jobs is famous for being extremely innovative, courageous and successful. As a result, many people might think that fear was not part of his life. However, if you read his biography you learn about all the times he was scared and unsure of himself or his decisions. The same is true for every entrepreneur - there is never a shortage of fear, risk and self-doubt. But something else makes them strive on.

Earlier I mentioned the huge career shift I made, leaving a corporate job in advertising and becoming an instructor for Outward Bound. That career change was by far the scariest big decision I've ever made and I procrastinated making it for ages. But luckily my courage finally kicked in. The huge changes and long list of unknowns that were now part of my life were very frightening, but I found the courage because what I wanted (more job fulfillment, better sense of a life purpose, more adventure, more impact) was greater than the fear. Not by much, but a bit. And that's why we do it...

Courage is being scared and doing
it anyway, because the something you
want is bigger than the fear itself.

In the context of this book, we need to be willing to be courageous in order to build a life that's right for us, because a life that is right for us is way more fulfilling and awesome than one that is not. So our "want" for that life needs to be bigger than the fear we will experience in order to get it.

On one of my many skydives, I was jumping with someone who had done over 1000 jumps. I asked him if he still got scared. He smiled, paused, and said, "Yep. Every single time. If I ever stop being scared I'll stop jumping, because then it won't serve a purpose for me."

Empowerment

Being courageous and facing fears also makes you feel *in control*. This is extremely empowering. You may not feel terribly *confident* in the moment, but you aren't allowing fear to dictate your decisions. Any time you avoid doing something you want to do simply because of fear, you are giving power to the fear. You are disempowering yourself. So, even though courage feels terrible in the moment because fear is involved, know that you are empowering yourself. You are doing what's right for *you*.

After that tear-filled first drive following the car accident, I felt an *immense* sense of empowerment. The sadness and fear was obviously still there, but I had faced it head on. That kept me in control of my life, not allowing fear to control it for me.

Think of the relief you feel *after* you have a difficult conversation with someone or after you finish an important project. Courage only feels good once the scary, courageous moment is over. At that point it feels phenomenal.

This desire to be in control of our lives and feel empowered permeates everything because for most of human history we couldn't control much! Control feels safe. Do you get an icky feeling when the sink is full of dirty dishes or your house is a mess? You don't feel in control. Why do some people put a nice little fence around their house and make sure the grass doesn't get too long? It makes them feel in control. Controlling as much as you can in life makes you feel better about the stuff that feels OUT of your control. Later on we'll take a look at how you can find control in *every* situation.

You are braver than you believe

At the same time, we routinely *underestimate* our courage because we mainly notice moments in life when we're scared, not when we're comfortable. One of my clients complained to me that she lacked courage and every opportunity frightened her. "Why am I such a chicken-shit?" she asked me. I pointed out that she had moved to Canada by herself from the Caribbean, knowing nobody when she arrived because all her friends and family were back home. This is a supremely courageous act that most people would be terrified of but she had completely forgotten about it.

Exercise

How have you been courageous in the past? How are you courageous now? How would your friends say you've been courageous? Believe me, they think you're brave at something.

Unfortunately the one time in a person's life when their friends and family say incredibly great things about them is at their funeral. When they can't hear it! I sit at funerals, listening to everyone talk about how awesome the person was and I think to myself, "I sure hope they heard this stuff when they were alive."

So while you're thinking about the courageous things you've done and continue to do, let someone close to you know how courageous you think THEY are. Chances are they take it for granted too and think nothing of it. But damn it feels good when someone tells you. Don't wait until their funeral when they can't hear it. Tell them now.

What does Mr Smart say?

Albert Einstein once said "If you have an hour to solve a problem, spend the first 55 minutes making sure you know exactly what the problem is, then spend 5 minutes solving it."

So if fear is at the root of why courageous acts are so difficult, we need to understand fear first, otherwise we don't know what we're dealing with.

But too often in life we are pushed, from inside or out, to get to the *solution* as soon as possible, because our world demands results. "Haven't you finished that yet? What's taking you so long?" As a result, we don't spend enough time making sure we're solving the *right* thing. Instead we do do do (take action), not dig dig dig (to get clear on what's really needed). But it is much more important to do the *right* thing, than it is to do things right. If you do a half-ass job at the right thing, you'll get better results than if you do the wrong thing perfectly.

I injured my knee a few years ago and noticed after a few

months that the knee was still sore. So I started doing exercises to build up the muscles surrounding my knee. Months went by but the pain continued. I finally went to a physiotherapist who told me the problem resulted from my BUTT muscles not being strong enough (insert image of flabby butt here). Apparently it's all connected - who knew?! This is a perfect example of not diagnosing a problem properly (weak butt) and thereby heading off onto a course of action (strengthening the leg muscles) that did not get me where I wanted to go. We do this all the time in all areas of our life. Have you ever accepted a new job, only to eventually discover it wasn't right for you? A lack of clarity could have been the reason.

So let's invite fear in, take a good hard look at it, wrestle with it a bit, slap it around a few times, and see what we can learn from it in order to get you on your journey of building a courageous life that's perfect for you.

" 'Can a man still be brave if he's afraid?'
'That is the only time a man can be brave,'
his father told him."

A Game of Thrones

Conclusions

Getting Clear On Courage

Courage is hard because it can't exist without fear.

To understand courage we first
have to understand fear.

Courage is being scared and doing it anyway
(because of a bigger want).

Courageous people never stop feeling scared.

Courage only feels good after the scary thing is over.

ON FEAR

"There are two basic motivating forces: fear and love.
When we are afraid, we pull back from life."
John Lennon

What is Fear?

Fear is defined as "a distressing emotion aroused by
impending danger, evil, pain, whether the threat is real or
imagined."

So why do we get scared? Where does that horrible feeling
come from that makes us want to scream, run, freeze or pee
our pants?

Unfortunately there is no shortage of things to be scared of.
There are hundreds of types of phobias (an extreme or
irrational fear) which, if extreme enough, can completely
hijack your ability to think. If anyone in the audience of one
of my keynote speeches is peladophobic, they won't retain a
word I say and they might even have nightmares about me.
Peladophobia is fear of bald people. Really? Me, scary? Come
on, I'm not so bad.

Where the heck does it come from?

We have inherited fear through evolution. For thousands and
thousands of years, we were scared daily when our life was in
physical danger. We were being hunted by a big hairy animal
that wanted to put us on its toast or we were being threatened
by unfriendly humans with sharp sticks. This fear kept us
alive; when we listened to it we were able to survive and pass

it on in our genes. We therefore came to rely on it. If you and your prehistoric buddy walked out of your cave one night and heard a rustling in the bushes, the person who got their ass back in the cave might survive to have children and pass on their survival fears. The person who got curious to wander over there and see what was making the cute rustling sound, didn't. That person's recklessness did not get passed on to future generations.

The same is true for animals at the bottom of the food chain. When a mouse or deer hears a noise, it doesn't stop to analyze the situation, it assumes the worst every single time. We do it too. This is the reason why when someone says something to you or about you and it's not perfectly clear what they mean, you will automatically assume the worst. Assuming the worst kept us alive for thousands of years and is therefore programmed into us. We may live in an online world but we have stone-age programming in our brains.

For thousands of years our fears taught us to avoid whatever was causing that yucky, fearful sensation in our gut. It is an instinctive response aimed at self-preservation.

This evolutionary programming can be seen every day. After a huge meal it can take your stomach 20 minutes to tell your brain that you're full. Why? Because for thousands of years we didn't get to eat every time we were hungry. Therefore when we got the chance to eat, our brain wanted us to absolutely stuff ourselves.

Our ancestors rarely got enough salt, sugar and fat in their diets since they were harder to find in nature, so they would always seek them out. Why do you think fast food is so enticing to us now? Salt, sugar and fat.

After watching a really scary movie do you ever stress about it actually happening to you? That's because until the camera was invented, every single thing human beings saw *had actually happened*. For most of human existence if you saw something, it was real! You remembered it clearly so you could use that information to survive. No matter how many times we tell ourselves that we won't ever be stuck on an airplane filled with killer snakes, if you've seen that movie then there is a part of your brain that actually believes it will happen. Because you saw it with your own eyes.

What is the face you make when you see or hear something absolutely disgusting? Make that face now. You probably crinkle up your nose and squint your eyes. You're doing that so you can't smell or see the yucky thing. Even if someone tells you something disgusting on the phone, you STILL make that face even though you can't actually see or smell what they're talking about. It is an automatic reaction that is programmed into you.

The Need to Belong

Our ability to survive long enough to get horny and pass on our genes so our kids can grow up and spend our inheritance isn't just limited to physical fears like animals, aggressive people and cliff edges. In order to survive we also had to be part of a group or "tribe". Humans cannot survive by themselves, they have to *belong* to a larger group of people. When a sea turtle is born it wiggles out of its shell, charges for the sea and starts swimming alone. We humans need a bit more assistance. We don't pop out of the womb, stand up, make dinner and find a job. We need to be cared for. Even as adults, for thousands of year we needed others for protection and for hunting. Being "cast out" of the tribe meant certain death.

As a result, this need to belong is our greatest need. Nothing gets in the way of you being 100% you more than your need to belong.

Story Time

I used to be a transition coach - helping people deal with getting fired. HR would have me wait in reception, the about-to-be-fired person would get walked down to a meeting room, told the bad news, then I would walk in to pick up the pieces. I'd spend the next few months helping them find a new job.

Their organization was a place where they had belonged but were now being told they didn't belong anymore. They weren't wanted. While most of them had some idea this day was coming (only once did I have a client who was completely blind-sided when he was laid off) it was still someone confirming they didn't want them around anymore. They now had to find a new company to belong to. While they had logistical concerns like "What will I do for money?" and "Where will I go next?" the predominate emotion was one of rejection. They felt hurt, alone, fragile and confused. They felt, at least temporarily, that they were no good. They no longer belonged.

If we feel we are not liked or if our social status is challenged, our brain processes it the same as if we just saw a bear in the woods charging towards us. Social harm is as threatening as physical harm. Plus, it's a helluva lot more common in our everyday lives unless you are on active duty in the military or you live in a volcano surrounded by starving lions.

Think of all the ways our social status can be challenged:
* When we don't get credit for something we've done.
* When we try something new with the possibility of failing and looking incompetent.

35

- When we feel we're not qualified.
- When we feel under-appreciated or disrespected.
- When we say something in a group and it's wrong.

An even more powerful threat to our social status occurs when someone tells us they don't want to be friends anymore or, even worse, our one-and-only breaks up with us. We are no longer part of the bigger group. And if you're getting dumped by your one-and-only, evolution is setting off ALL the warning lights in your brain because how the heck are you going to procreate and pass on your genes to future generations if you don't have a snuggle partner?

All of these things feed our fear that we won't belong, which convinces us we therefore cannot survive.

Belonging = Survival
Abandonment = Death

Yes, your social fears - like public speaking, failure, being laughed at, standing up for what you believe in, telling someone you're unhappy with them, or someone telling you they don't want you around anymore - all stem from nature's desire for you to be accepted by others so you can belong to a larger group and therefore survive.

Think of the sensation you get if you're sitting in a group of people and someone makes fun of you and everyone laughs. Your body reacts to the fear, possibly by increasing your temperature, making your palms a bit sweaty, and inevitably raising your heart-rate. You can't think clearly. Thousands of years of evolution start screaming at you, "This is bad, get away from here or do something about it *fast*."

The term in medical sociology is *social support*. Having it helps us stay happy and healthy, lacking it leaves us frail. Both psychological and physical health problems are more common among people who lack social attachments. It has been well documented that loneliness is one of the main causes of Alzheimer's.

In 2009 a US Army psychologist killed 13 people at an army base in Texas. It is believed his actions were due in part to his feeling of a lack of belonging. Such a lack of belonging - caused by rejection or social isolation - is associated with emotional distress, mental and physical illness, suicide, crime, and aggression.

Here are some of the most common negative emotions we can experience when a lack of belonging creeps into our present situation: abandoned, confused, disappointed, embarrassed, guilty, helpless, inferior, misunderstood, neglected, picked on, rejected, trapped, unconfident, worthless.

Yuck.

Fear is sneaky

Our fears want so badly for us to play it safe in life that we have even come up with a new, more acceptable word to use instead of 'fear'. We call it 'stress'.

Stress is fear in disguise.

For some reason we accept stress because saying "I'm stressed" doesn't make us look as bad as saying "I'm scared". For example…

- "I'm stressed about this presentation I'm giving tomorrow" might equal "I'm scared I'll screw it up."
- "I'm stressed about my job interview next week" might be masking "I'm scared I won't get the job or I'll seem

unprepared."

- "I'm stressed about all the work I have to do this week" may be "I'm scared I won't get it done on time, or if I do it might not be any good."
- "I'm stressed about seeing my family this weekend" might mean "I'm afraid they'll bug me about my lack of career or my boyfriend who they don't like."

For some reason, saying "I'm stressed" can make us feel busy and important. Saying "I'm scared" can make us feel weak.

Cavemen had acute stress (intense, in the moment) whereas we present-day humans have a lower level of stress which exists over longer periods of time. Nowadays, stress isn't like being attacked by a bear, it's more like being continually nagged by a mosquito. A mosquito with malaria.

Your brain on fear

When any of these social threats happen, the effect on us physically can be debilitating. Let's take a quick look, without getting too complex, at how fear can hijack your brain.

When it comes to fear there are two main parts of the brain. The old part which animals also have is the limbic area. The newer part is the prefrontal cortex. But let's use more common names for these two areas. Let's call the old part the "Emotional" brain and the newer part the "Rational" brain.

Regardless of the fears that you personally want to get a grip on in order to live a life true to yourself the way we handle these fears and learn to manage them is exactly the same because your brain can't tell the difference. All it knows is that you're scared and that is BAD.

When your Emotional brain perceives a threat it floods your Rational brain (where perceptions are formed and decisions are made) with adrenaline, *so you cannot think*. You literally can't think straight - your brain *doesn't want you to think* because for thousands of years if you took a moment to stop and think, you died. We sometimes hear people talk about Fight or Flight. This is the reaction that your emotional brain wants fear to initiate. Fight whatever is endangering you, or take Flight and get the heck away from it as fast as possible. That is what kept us alive for centuries.

A very common version of Fight in the modern world is when someone says something that insults or challenges you. Our heart-rate picks up and we often lash out with something equally not-nice. Evolution wants us to do that, but it is never in our best interest! If someone makes you angry and the first thing that comes out of your mouth feels good to say, it's wrong. Every time. Think about it.

The third reaction that fear can cause - in addition to Fight and Flight - is to Freeze. Very often we can be so scared that we literally stay still and are unable to talk. Freezing keeps many animals alive in times of danger because our predators' eyes are better at picking up things that are moving. While we humans can float between the various reactions - freezing sometimes or wanting to fight other times - I believe each of us is more inclined to one of the three reactions. I'm more inclined to feel a Fight reaction, whereas a close friend of mine is definitely more of a Freezer.

Think of when you get in a heated argument with someone, then 5 minutes later you imagine all the perfect things you SHOULD have said, but couldn't find the words in the moment. "If I had said THIS, that really would have shown him." That moment when you can't seem to find the words is an example of your rational brain being hijacked.

Your heart-rate can increase from 60 to 150 beats almost immediately. Your temperature goes through the roof, your palms get sweaty and your throat gets dry. At the same time your senses seem to heighten. Blood actually rushes to your hands so you can pick up a weapon or punch someone. Your inner cave man or woman just hopped in a time machine and is now sitting in your brain, handling the controls and hitting the Fight, Flight or Freeze buttons.

Flickr: nightmaresfearfactory

This photo is from a haunted house. These people know rationally they won't actually die or be hurt but when fear is involved our rational brain takes a nap. Look at the evolutionary programming that is evident here: their eyes are wide open to take in as much information as possible, their mouths are open to show their teeth and they're screaming in order to alert anyone nearby who might be able to help (and also to scare off the approaching danger), plus they're backing up and grabbing on to each other for protection.

Within a second they will remember where they are and what they're doing and they will relax and laugh. But in that initial moment, their emotional brain controls everything. As Plato said, "We must use the reins of rationale on the horse of emotion."

What I hope you're starting to understand now is that you are 100% normal if you experience fear. You were programmed that way.

You are not alone

Whatever you're scared of in your day-to-day life, thousands of other people are scared of it too. Whatever "it" is. With my experience coaching hundreds of people of all ages and backgrounds, it is amazing how similar we all are when it comes to fear and courage. Most of the fears you have are shared by every other person. When you're sitting in a group, afraid to raise your hand and state your opinion, other people in the room are scared of the same thing. Most people just never admit it!

Have you experienced walking into a social setting and realizing you don't know anyone and you're not sure who to talk to and you feel like everyone's watching you? Most people feel this every single time! For some people this is as frightening as jumping out of a plane. But in reality, the people you approach are just as scared as you are because they're worried about saying the wrong thing too. They're worried you'll think they're not smart. They're worried you're more *interesting* than they are.

You know that feeling when you're single and you see a cute person on the other side of the room who you think maybe, possibly, might have just looked at you a few minutes ago? And you want to strut over there and say hi but you feel like as soon as you try to talk your stomach is going to come out your mouth? MOST PEOPLE GET THAT!

People who know me well think I am courageous to the point of craziness. They think I'm scared of nothing. They're wrong. I'm simply an expert on courage and for years I've put into practice the ideas and habits in this book. Remember, courage isn't about not being scared, it's about being scared and doing it anyway. So yes, I am very courageous because I face my fears, but here are some of the many things I'm very scared of: not being liked, other people thinking I'm not smart, thinking I'm not tough, thinking I'm not unique, not being a "success" in my life, feeling like I'm wasting my days and not being productive enough, scared of getting old and not being attractive, scared of not wearing the right clothes to an event and feeling out of place, scared of looking like a complete loser when I sneeze all over myself during allergy season.... I could go on and on and on.

So cut yourself some slack. EVERYbody gets scared from time to time. If you're never scared, it means you are coasting through life, not maximizing your gifts, and not living true to the person that you're meant to be. If you're never scared, you are not being you.

When were *you* last scared?

"Everything you want is on the other side of fear."
Jack Canfield

The #1 Fear – "The Big & Nasty"

You're still reading this book? Even after all that fear talk? That proves you have all the courage you need to put this stuff into reality and turbo-charge your life.

All that talk about fear, social fears, belonging blah blah is a lot to remember, right? Well here is where we get really simple. We are going to distil all those social fears down to the real culprit; the one single fear that is at the root of our need to belong. Are you ready? This fear holds you, me and everyone else back from living our biggest, boldest life. I call it the Big & Nasty Fear.

Story Time

I've always had a fear of not being unique or special. I always thought people liked me because I was different and independent. I do things differently than most and I get more out of life than most people do. And I'm proud of that. I've always been scared that if I got married then people would think I was "settling down". They might think I had lost the edge I was always so proud of. That fear held me back until I became aware of it. Awareness is always the first step.

I was also scared the ring would fall through the crack in the floor of the elevator (I proposed to her in the exact elevator where we had first met 3.5 years earlier) but the real fear was "Will people think I'm not unique and independent if I 'settle down' and get married?"

The Big & Nasty Fear = "What will people think of me?"

I have seen this fear screw up relationships, jobs, marriages,

43

careers and overall happiness and performance. That's right, we are ALL scared of what other people think of us.

Obviously I'm talking about *negative* stuff that people think of us. Positive stuff is quite yummy for our well-being. If you think I'm the smartest, cutest guy you've ever met in your life, that is not going to hurt my happiness one bit. It's going to make me feel like a million dollars after tax, thank you very much. But when someone might think *negatively* of us, when they might *judge* us poorly, all the warning bells in our brain go off and we start to panic because maybe we won't belong.

How does the Big & Nasty make you *feel?* I call feelings the "f-word" because most people don't like to talk about them. Most of us would rather sew our face to the carpet than risk the feeling we get when we're poorly judged by other people.

I have worked with a range of people from 14-year-olds struggling to fit in at school to 60-year-old CEO's struggling to decide how to spend the next million dollars, people who came from a poor upbringing in a rough neighborhood to private-school kids who seemed to have it easy (though this was rarely the case). Regardless of who it is, the Big & Nasty holds them back from living their unique life and dealing with challenges. It held me back again and again in my life.

Exercise

Go back to the unhappy list you wrote down earlier. Take a look at it again and ask yourself, "What would be different if I didn't care what other people thought of me?" The Big & Nasty will affect some areas more than others, but if you really dig deep you will see it is involved with most of them.

A humorous look at The Big & Nasty

I'm always entertained by men's behavior in the gym locker room. It's the perfect recipe for social insights; a mixture of stereotypical manliness ("pumping iron" and looking buff) with a host of non-stereotypical manliness like walking around other half-naked guys.

For example, a 20-something man removes his underwear and puts a towel around his waist, and in so doing clears his throat or coughs two or three times, louder than usual, and perhaps slams his locker door a little harder than he needs to in order to assert his manliness. The moisturizer dispenser might as well not be there because many guys can't flex enough to make up for that blatant disregard of toughness. Some men would prefer to have skin that's dryer than an elephant's scrotum in the middle of the Serengeti rather than apply a slightly aromatic skin product.

In the sauna the younger men sit AS FAR AWAY from each other as possible. If one person leaves and they're suddenly stuck sitting too close to the only other guy in the sauna, one of them will make a deep cough and casually shift away while feeling the need to say "No offence, man."

The only men who consistently do their own thing are the old guys. The closer to death they are, the less they seem to care about anyone else. They are secure in who they are and don't give a hoot what anyone thinks. They'll walk around the locker-room whistling and strutting their naked stuff even if their private parts resemble a button on a fur coat. They just don't care!

Imagine having this attitude EARLIER in life? Why wait until you're old and wrinkly? Imagine having the guts to be 100% you and not worry about other people's opinions. That would feel like a huge weight off your shoulders, no?

Hang on, isn't failure the biggest fear?

Many people believe failure is the biggest limiting fear, but it's not - we just convince ourselves it is.

Put up your hand if you've ever sung in the shower. Go on, put it up, even though I can't see you. We all know you've done it. Now, would you be willing to sing the national anthem at the Super Bowl in front of millions of viewers?

Most people, when asked this question, vigorously shake their heads and get a look on their face like they just saw Jaws come out of their toilet. But your singing voice is the same in the soapy confines of your shower as it is in the middle of a packed stadium with overpriced beer. Your voice is just as bad, or good, in the shower as it would be out there, but you don't care in the shower, do you? Why? Because no one is there to *judge* you!

When I dance at a bar or a wedding, I dance safe. When I dance at home by myself, I dance like a mad-man on Red Bull.

Would you be comfortable walking down the street naked (assuming it wasn't illegal)? Most people would not. But do you mind walking around your bedroom naked by yourself with the blinds closed? You're just as naked in your room as you would be on the street, and you look the same. But no one is judging you at home.

Failure on its own doesn't scare us so much. It's the possibility of failing in *front of other people*. "What will they *think* of me?!" They may not respect you, they may think you're not smart, not cool, and they may not want to hang out with you. You won't belong.

Story Time

I once led a group of international volunteers in Vanuatu, a country in the South Pacific near Fiji. I was working for an international aid organization and we had 10 weeks to build a school for a poor community.

It turned out to be the most mentally draining experience of my entire life so far. We had serious internal conflict with some of the volunteers and my co-leader never showed up. Five weeks in, we decided as a group to end the project. We left the school unfinished. We were simply so drained that we didn't feel we could continue. I was close to tears I was so spent.

As a leader I had done the best I could with a bad situation but, in the end, we had not finished what we set out to do. I had failed the people of the island and the people on my team.

The failure was tough but I knew the islanders would easily be able to finish building the school themselves. We had done the hardest part and we had provided them with the supplies they needed to continue. But I realized I was most concerned with what they now thought of me as a person. Did they think I was a bad leader? Did the Chief of the island who had adopted me as his son no longer respect me? Would the islanders think that all Canadians were quitters? What would I tell my friends when I got back home? Would the organization I was representing not want to work with me again?

Failure isn't the culprit. It's the fear of what others will think of us if we fail.

Your Fear Filter

How does the Big & Nasty affect our everyday lives?

Imagine you've just started a new job. You're nervous because everything is unfamiliar. But you want to impress everyone so they think positively of you, proving that hiring you was a good decision. You want to show you're smart enough and you can add value and therefore prove that you belong there. In other words, you don't want to fail and get fired.

At your first chance to speak up and share your opinion, you do it! You say what's on your mind even though your heart-rate quickens and your ego is saying "Shut-up for god's sake, they might think you're dumb." Your boss listens to your input, thinks for a second, then says in front of the entire group, "That's an *interesting* point of view."

Interesting? What the hell does she mean by *that*? For the next five minutes you stress about all the different things that word can mean. Your ears may have heard "That's an interesting point of view" but because you're new on the job, nervous about fitting in and making a great first impression, your ego hears "What a stupid idea. You're new here, right? Maybe we shouldn't have hired you. You might as well start packing your bags right now."

Welcome to the world of your Filter. We think we see and hear the world as it is, but we do not.

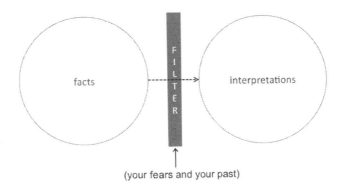

(your fears and your past)

"Facts" (on the left) are the things that actually happen in life. But as in the above example, we don't always recognize them. Everything we see and hear goes through our filter and comes out the other end as our Interpretation. We are constantly interpreting. Have you ever had someone say something to you, taken it as an insult, lost your cool, only to have that person look completely surprised and hurt because they didn't mean what you think you heard? Have you ever received a text message or email that made you angry or upset, approached the subject, only to realize you had it all wrong?

This happens to everyone. You. Me. Everyone.

Your filter is made up of two main things: 1) the fears we all share, and 2) your past. This book is focused on #1. #2 (how the experiences from your past are getting in your way) is a bit too complex for a book to help you uncover. It is best dealt with through deeper self-awareness experiences like 1-on-1 coaching, therapy, or group workshops such as The Landmark Forum.

So, facts happen in life, then we put them through our filter unknowingly, and our interpretation comes out the other side. Sometimes your interpretation is accurate and matches the fact. Often times it is WAY off.

F.E.A.R.

But here's the tricky bit. Because our brains are so focused on self-preservation, it tries to convince us that anything that evokes fear with even the SLIGHTEST chance of happening will for-sure happen, no doubt about it.

But in actuality, most fears never come to fruition. A great acronym for fear is **F**alse **E**xpectations **A**ppearing **R**eal. We convince ourselves the fear is real because it gives us a super excuse to avoid it!

> "I am an old man and have known a great many troubles, but most of them have never happened."
> *Mark Twain*

So how do you know whether or not to act on a fear? How do we know if it is a legitimate fear versus our filter trying to protect our ego? We'll dig into that later in this book.

That voice in your head

We spoke already about how fear shows up physically in your body. You will always *feel* it before you *understand* rationally what's going on.

But in case the physical sensations of fear weren't already enough to stress us out, there is something else that exists in all of us which works as hard as it possibly can to keep us from doing anything remotely scary. It's a voice in your head.

That's right, a voice. Any time you have an opportunity to be courageous, that voice jumps into your head and says things like, "Hang on, is this a good idea? This isn't going to end well. You're going to mess this up. What will people think? You're not smart enough to do this. You're not good enough!"

Story Time

One of my executive coaching clients (we'll call him Jim), had just landed a new job; a big job as Vice President of a large company. He was getting paid big bucks and he had a heck of a lot of responsibility. Soon after he started he attended the staff Christmas party. The CEO got up and gave a speech to all the staff, introducing Jim, explaining his role and the millions of dollars he was going to raise for the organization. When he finished, everyone in the room turned to Jim and started clapping. They might have been thinking "Wow, this guy must be really bright and successful, what a huge responsibility he has. He must be super smart. But look at him – he looks so calm and in control."

Jim told me later how he was actually feeling at that point. He was sitting there smiling, looking confident and waving at everyone but thinking to himself, "What the $%# have I got myself into? How am I going to do this?! I never should have taken this job! I'm going to screw it up. They're all looking at me. I'm going to fail!"

Pretty harsh, isn't it? Welcome to the world of your Inner Critic - the voice of all those fears we've been talking about, hammering away at your ideas and your self-worth. It will keep you from getting what you want and being the person you're meant to be. It is a persistently negative voice in your head that wants you to live a safe and boring life. It even distorts reality in order to get its way. It is often referred to as your "ego". I prefer to call it the Inner Critic because that is what it constantly does - criticizes. If left unchecked, the Inner Critic will have us consistently perform below our potential.

The good news is that EVERYBODY has this voice. Yes, everybody. Even the most daring, seemingly-fearless person. It shows up when we 1) try something scary, 2) *consider* trying something scary, 3) simply *hear* of an opportunity to try something scary.

Anyone who claims not to have this voice in their head is either lying or living life so safe that the voice doesn't show up very much. But it's still there.

You're not nuts

When I first learned of the Inner Critic I was extremely relieved. "You mean, I'm not crazy and I don't need to be put in a padded cell, strapped down to a bed? Hmmm, this is quite excellent news." Until then I never had the guts to ask someone else if they had that voice too. My clients experience this as well and often say, "Really? It's not just me? Phew!"

The Inner Critic is simply the result of evolution, wanting us to grab a drink, a bag of chips, and plop down in a comfy chair in the middle of our comfort zone and never leave it. Remember, for thousands of years the avoidance of fear kept us alive; if your life wasn't in danger and you weren't starving to death, you were doing everything you needed to survive so why push it? Your Inner Critic wants nothing to change, wants you to follow habits and patterns and never wants to feel the potential stress and anxiety that comes with trying something scary. It wants you to be safe and boring.

What does YOURS say?

While everyone's Inner Critic says something similar, you also have something very specific that it says just to you. It's based on your past, especially your childhood, and it makes up the second part of the Fear Filter ("your past"). In the world of self-awareness, it is one of the most important things you can know about yourself.

My Inner Critic says all the typical stuff like everyone else's does, but the specific, most potent thing that mine says to me is this: "You're not smart enough, you're not professional enough, people won't take you seriously."

What's good about it?

If we approach the Inner Critic correctly, it can become our guardian angel and the key to a more kick-ass life. We can eventually feel GOOD when we hear that voice. Why? Because every time it shows up in your head it is a sign that you have an *opportunity* to push yourself and grow.

When I was a kid I went by the name Billy. Then as I reached my teenage years I felt like I had to get serious so I switched to Bill (as most Billy's eventually do). But when I had my identity crisis at 30 years old and left my advertising career I realized that Billy was way more fitting for the real me. For me, "Bill" was playing it safe and living by everyone else's rules. So I switched back to Billy. I named my Inner Critic "Bill". It tries to make me conform and take the safest route every time.

Not many Bills start going by Billy in their 30's, but it felt right for me!

Exercise

When you're out of your comfort zone, what does your Inner Critic say to you? Imagine being in the kind of social situation that would make you uncomfortable, anxious, or downright horrified.

How can we manage it?

We will never fully control our Inner Critic but we can take steps to *manage* it. Step 1 is for me to acknowledge that Bill is there, because every problem we ignore just gets bigger. "Oh hi Bill, nice to see you." Step 2 is to say "Thanks for showing up Bill and reminding me that I have a chance here to step out of my comfort zone." Step 3 is to ask Bill why he's all worked up: "What are you trying to protect me from? Are you helping me or holding me back?" Step 4 is to say, "I appreciate your input Bill and I've considered it. This is what I'm choosing to do."

Step 5 is to feel fantastic because you looked fear in the eye and told it where to go. DAMN that's empowering, plus your courage and confidence just got a boost of energy!
I encourage you to name your Inner Critic and have that kind

of conversation with him/her the next time it shows up. Have some fun picking an Inner Critic name that really works for you – I've heard some doozies!

Exercise

What name would you give YOUR Inner Critic?

The Inner Critic shows up all over the place. For example, I know many professionals who don't think people take them seriously in their job because their university degree (which they got more than 20 years ago) isn't related to what they're doing now. So they assume their co-workers think they're a fake, even though no one else in the company even knows their history!

I know someone who is terrified to talk about the f-word (feelings) at work because when he opened up emotionally to a friend in grade 5, the popular kids told him he was weird and they made fun of him. It's still affecting his behavior now that he is the director of a company!

When I was in grade 8, one of the cool kids made fun of how I dressed and to this day (almost 30 years later) I still fuss about what I'm going to wear sometimes.

Those things never leave us and they negatively affect how we interpret the world around us. So how do we let go of it? You've already started: simply being aware that it's happening and trying not to let it take over your life. Have that conversation with your Inner Critic when it shows up. You will gradually be less and less impacted by its voice.

Conclusions

Getting Clear on Fear

Fear is normal. You're normal.

Fear will always exist when you're being courageous.

The number 1 fear that holds you back from being you is the fear of what others will think of you. It's the Big & Nasty!

Your fear filter decides how you interpret what happens.

Your Inner Critic tries to convince you to take the safe, non-scary option even when it might not be right for you in the long-run.

ON INCREASING COURAGE

---

*"We must build dikes of courage to
hold back the flood of fear."*
Martin Luther King, Jr.

Can we make it easier?

"So Billy, what you're saying is that I need courage to get a life that's right for me as opposed to the life others expect of me. But since courage involves fear, it's going to be scary, right?"

Oh goody.

But here's the good news. It is possible to get more comfortable with being courageous and facing fear, even though thousands of years of evolution are telling you to play it safe.

That's where we're headed now. At the end of this section you will understand how to become a more courageous person so you can immediately start being the ballsy you who lives the life you want to live. We'll start by looking at some pretty circles.

These three circles represent Comfort Zones and they are at the root of seeing how courage can be made easier. The way these 3 circles interact is crucial to you becoming more courageous and thereby grabbing your life by the you-know-whats.

In order to keep this section of the book from sounding too theoretical, we'll use a very common example of fear to see what we can learn from it: the fear of public speaking. This is one of the most common fears in the world and even if you do it for a living like I do there is always a bit of fear involved, especially as you talk to larger and larger audiences.

Note: Since you already understand fear, you know it's not really the fear of public speaking that you're scared of, is it? It's the fear of what people will think of you if you screw it up!

Imagine you're sitting amongst a group of people with whom you feel comfortable. Friends, classmates, or work colleagues. Since you know and trust these people well, you are presently in your Comfort Zone (the inner circle) where you don't feel scared, stressed or anxious in any way. Sitting on your couch watching TV or walking down the street in a neighborhood you know well are other examples. A very large chunk of our daily lives is spent in the Comfort Zone.

Then someone in the group mentions an upcoming opportunity to speak in front of a large gathering of people. A very important group of people. A very smart group of people. "Which of you would like to volunteer to do this talk?"

Even just the *mention* of this scary opportunity makes your heart-rate speed up and your temperature rise a bit as you look around the room hoping no one will single you out. You're not in your Comfort Zone anymore. Just the *thought* of doing this scary thing makes you uncomfortable and you are therefore in the second circle, the Courage Zone. We could call it the fear zone but we want to feel empowered so we call it the Courage Zone. And since being courageous is scary, fear lives here.

This can happen while we're in the middle of something scary (walking up to the stage to speak) but more commonly the fear is felt BEFORE we do the scary thing. Just the *thought* of it puts us out of our comfort zone.

There is a chance that your fear of public speaking is SO big that you have skipped right over the Courage Zone and made a one-way trip to the outer circle, the Panic Zone. You are in your Panic Zone when something is so scary and stressful that you can't even think straight. It absolutely terrifies you and may even make you feel like barfing.

If this kind of big speaking opportunity was offered to you, what zone would YOU be in? In the Courage Zone or the Panic Zone? If this is something that only scares you a little bit because you've done loads of speaking before, then perhaps you're just barely in the Courage Zone, not too far from the Comfort Zone. However, if this scares you quite a bit, perhaps you're at the far edge of the Courage Zone, flirting with the Panic Zone. OR, if speaking in public scares you more than anything you can ever imagine, you might be so overcome with dread that you're at the outer edge of the Panic Zone.

The Panic Zone is NOT where you want to be. This is where the old part of your brain (emotion) is so freaked out that it sends adrenaline to the rational part of your brain, in order to muddle it up so you can't even think straight. The Panic Zone is not a productive place to be. You want to avoid it.

Wherever you are is perfect

It's crucial to note that there is no right or wrong zone. We're all different. Imagine two people; we'll call them Fred and Fran. Fred is a father of three and has never spoken in front of a large audience. The idea terrifies him. Fran, on the other hand, speaks regularly to big groups at work, but has very little experience with kids and feels she doesn't have a clue how to talk to them. An opportunity to speak in front of a huge group puts Fran only slightly out into her Courage Zone but puts Fred WAY into his Panic Zone. However, the idea of taking care of the neighbor's kids for the weekend has Fred firmly in his Comfort Zone while it puts Fran knee deep in her Panic Zone.

The point is this: some activities are frightening for some people, while not for others. I am more comfortable jumping out of a plane compared to all my friends who haven't done it, but there are other things they're more comfortable doing than I am. Just because an opportunity puts you farther out of your comfort zone than it does for someone else, it doesn't mean they're a braver person than you are. There is probably something else that scares them that you're more comfortable with. Try not to compare yourself to others when it comes to courage! If an opportunity scares you, then it is a courageous act, whether or not it scares anyone else.

Courage is Relative

Story Time

I was once leading a high-ropes activity for an Outward Bound Canada course. The activity entailed climbing up a short ladder, hooking up to a hanging rope, then getting winched up by your team-mates approximately 30 feet off the ground where you would then release yourself to swing at a very high speed. Scary to say the least. The first participant had done this activity a bunch of times so he went right to the top, pulled the lever, then swung through the air like Tarzan, cheering all the way.

Then a 65-year-old female participant only made it to the second step on the ladder. She could only go about 1 foot off the ground, with no chance of getting hooked in, winched up and swinging through the air. But for her, that was twice as terrifying as it was for the previous guy who went all the way to the top. Therefore SHE was showing the most courage.

Measuring your own courage has nothing to do with what actions you choose to do, it has to do with how scared you are when you do it. When it comes to courage, don't compare yourself to the actions of others, compare yourself to the level of courage it takes you to do the action. A bungee-jumper is not necessarily being more courageous than someone who jumps into the water off of a 5-foot cliff. The more courageous one is the one who is the most scared but does it anyway.

Even if something *appears* to be courageous, if the person doing it isn't scared, it's not courage. Jumping out of an airplane the first time is uber courageous for every single person who does it, but the 100th jump isn't terribly courageous because it's way less scary.

Recently I gave a talk to a crowd of volunteers on International Volunteer Day. I speak for a living, so I was only a bit scared (I get nervous 5 minutes before I start, then it goes away completely as soon as I'm on stage). Therefore I was only being a bit courageous. Alternatively, if you are terrified of speaking in public, but you get up there anyway, you are being WAY more courageous than I am in that moment. Whether or not you ace it or you stutter and splutter the whole time, it still counts for courage! You are doing it *despite* your fear, not allowing it to control your life and hold you back.

I once tried stand-up comedy. It was one of the scariest things I've ever done. The pressure to be up there in front of all those people and make them LAUGH? I was being extremely courageous and I know that because I was absolutely terrified. So terrified I didn't realize how much I was drinking before it was my turn to be up on stage (the event was held at a bar). When I finally got up there to the microphone I stood there gazing out at the audience and I realized, "Oh no. I'm *wrecked.*" Not sure if it helped or not, but I don't recommend it.

Even if no one else you know is scared of doing it, it still counts as courage for you if you're scared. So stop judging your courage by comparing yourself to others. I guarantee you many people pretend to be more courageous than they are. From all the clients I have worked with, EVERYONE has fears and they're not very different from one person to the next. And if you know someone who says they're never scared or they don't fear anything, that person is either a) lying, or b) not pushing themselves in their life. If you are never scared, then I would say you are coasting through life and wasting your days.

How do we make it easier?

Imagine you start a new job that entails you presenting to the senior management team once a month. But you're still kind of young and inexperienced. The thought of presenting is terrifying. The first time you do it you may sweat right through your shirt and feel like fainting. You are so far into the Courage Zone that you're dangerously close to the Panic Zone. Maybe it even feels like you've got one foot in the Panic Zone. But imagine you do this weekly for a year. How different will it be by year-end? As you can imagine, it will get a tiny bit easier every single time, until the fear almost disappears.

This is how all challenges begin. At first we are WAY into our Courage Zone, but each time we do it we slowly move back towards the Comfort Zone until we're knee-deep in it and the stress goes away. We have transformed the fear into a level of comfort by repeated exposure.

The more we confront that which scares us, the less it will continue to scare us over time.

Speaking in front of others, meeting new people, trying out for a team or joining a club, sharing our thoughts and feelings with others…. The more we do it, the easier it gets. This is because courage is a *muscle*.

Courage is a Muscle

Courage is not stagnant. You are not born with a set amount of it and stuck with it for life. How courageous you are a year from now is 100% in YOUR control. The more you flex your courage muscle by stepping out of your Comfort Zone, the bigger your courage grows and the easier it will be next time.

The muscles in your body don't grow and get stronger overnight. It takes consistent trips to the gym over a long period of time. You have to have patience and heaps of perseverance to grow a muscle to the point where you see a difference. Courage is no different. The more you step out of your Comfort Zone the quicker and bigger your courage muscle will get. Over time, your Comfort Zone grows and the Panic Zone shrinks. The things that used to scare you no longer do (or at least, not as much). The things you once considered to be impossible may now seem within your reach.

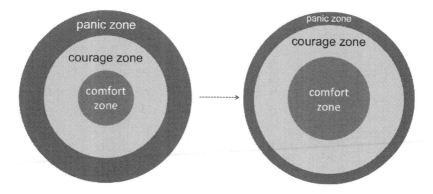

As Aldous Huxley said, "Every ceiling, when reached, becomes a floor upon which one walks." Every fearful opportunity that seems completely out of your grasp will eventually feel more comfortable as you face the fear. You will then be amazed at how much anxiety the thought of it used to cause you.

Just like a muscle, your courage needs to continue to be exercised. You can go to the gym for a year and be in the best shape of your life, but what happens if you stop going? You go back to the way you were. You don't get to a high level of courage and then stay there without continually exercising it. The good news, though, is the concept of muscle memory. If you take a break and then get back into it, you will return to your previous level quicker than it took you to get there the first time.

A study by Gardner & Bell in 2005 describes the benefits of exposure to fear: "Only by gradually exposing ourselves to the feared stimulus, albeit in a controlled and supported way, can we make significant progress in the recovery process. Just as a patient with a pulled muscle is advised to stretch gently to the point of discomfort but not to pain, so a phobic sufferer must enter a process of desensitization through exposure. This process is accomplished in small increments that combine bearable discomfort with feelings of progress and achievement. No phobic sufferer has to metaphorically or literally leap in to a snake pit or wallow in worms to attack phobia successfully."

Taking small steps to face your fears grows your Comfort Zone and shrinks your Panic Zone, making you more courageous and ready to take on bigger challenges.

For courage's sake

This book is focused on having the courage to live a life that's true to you. That means Taking Action in the areas of your life which you want to change or improve. That is *proactive* action towards a specific goal. For example, perhaps you want to be more comfortable with expressing your opinion, saying no to people or taking on more challenges at work. For this you need to repeatedly step out of your Comfort Zone *in that particular area*. You need to continually expose yourself to THAT specific fear. For meeting other people, you need to continually put yourself in scenarios to *meet new people*. To be more comfortable with public speaking, you need to speak in public.

However, you can also work towards growing your *general* courage muscle so it is more readily available when you need it. This is done by finding ways to be out of your Comfort Zone in any area of your life, thereby getting more used to the feeling of being scared and acting anyway. Your brain and body gets more comfortable with the sensation of being scared, choosing to face the fear anyway, and then experiencing the positive sensations and emotions once it's over. Whether you're about to jump off a high diving board or you're about to tell a joke to people you've never met before, your brain just knows that you were scared and you did it anyway. It adds the courageous event to your internal database that says "See? You *are* courageous!"

What you're actually doing with all this courage practice is building new neural pathways in your brain. It's just like a path in the wilderness - the more times you walk it, the easier it gets to follow. Modern research has demonstrated that the brain continues to create new neural pathways and alter existing ones in order to adapt to new experiences, learn new information and create new memories.

This means that in terms of our overall level of courage, every opportunity to face a fear can grow our courage muscle. While there are many ways to be courageous at work, there are often risks involved in that environment because we can only mess up so many times before we commit a CLM (Career Limiting Move). It can often be safer to use our personal life on a regular basis to get accustomed to the courage experience.

Later in this book we will focus more on very specific ways to practice courage to get the life you want, but for now let's dive into this idea of building your generic courage muscle in safe environments, thereby strengthening that muscle, building new neural pathways, and having some fun!

Story Time

When I was a fundraising director for a large international charity, I had a volunteer who was intrigued with my work on courage. She claimed to be scared of everything and she didn't like how it was dictating her life. It kept her from being her. So she asked me for help. Together we came up with a way for her to step out of her Comfort Zone in a safe way. A way that would put her well into her Courage Zone, but not quite her Panic Zone. Her challenge: make a Facebook profile.

That's right. The thought of having a Facebook profile terrified her. "But then I'll be on the INTERNET! People will SEE me!" Whether or not this scares the majority of people is irrelevant - it scared her so it was a perfect place to start flexing her courage muscle.

The next day she came into my office with a huge smile on her face saying, "I did it! I'm on the Internet! I feel so good - what can I do next?!" She looked like she just saw Santa come down the chimney, she was so excited. And she was PROUD of herself because she felt in control. The challenge that had seemed so scary to her the day before (getting on Facebook) was complete and now she wanted more. "What can I do next?!" So we decided on her next Comfort-Zone-expanding challenge: she would try to start a conversation with the person beside her on the bus, once a week.

This is the beauty - there are a multitude of opportunities to grow your overall courage muscle. I do it all the time. Some of the more typical fear-facing activities I've done include bungee-jumping, stand-up comedy, hang-gliding, swimming with sharks, sleeping in the middle of the wilderness alone in two feet of snow. But daily life has many opportunities too, as my Facebooking volunteer showed. When I'm on public transportation I try to start a conversation with the person beside me. My Inner Critic shouts, "No, don't do it! They'll think you're hitting on them! They'll think you're creepy! What will the other people around you think?!"

Even for a guy who jumps out of planes, I get a little flutter of fear every time I start a conversation with a stranger. And I do it because I know that courage is a muscle and the more I use it, the better I get at it.

Story Time

When I do a keynote on courage and fear, I have one story that no one forgets. One year I was flying across the country to visit my brother. It was a week before Halloween so he dared me to wear a costume on the plane. Immediately my heart started pounding as I contemplated being on a plane, alone, wearing a costume when nobody else was. But then I thought, "Hey, this is a perfect opportunity to build my courage muscle. What can I wear that will put me as close as possible to my Panic Zone?"

This picture was taken minutes before the taxi came to pick me up and take me to the airport. I flew 5 hours BY

 MYSELF wearing that outfit. It was one of the most terrifying (and fun) experiences of my life.

As I walked out of the house to the cab, I had to pass about 6 construction workers who were fixing the neighbor's roof. Their chins almost hit the pavement as they watched

me walk by. I began sweating. The cab driver told me that he almost drove off when he saw me.

As we approached the airport my heart-rate really started pounding! I walked into the packed airport and people immediately started staring and laughing. One person shouted, "It's a man!" Imagine how this felt?

I was so incredibly uncomfortable, but as is the case with all courageous acts, I also felt ALIVE! I felt empowered and in control. The ticket lady thought it was fantastic. The customs officer asked if I lost a bet. A girl approached me and loved my confidence so much she gave me her phone number.

My 5-hour seat was beside a deaf couple. They read my lips as I tried to explain why I was dressed that way. When I arrived ay my destination my brother took one look at me and immediately collapsed on the floor in a fit of laughter.

And I knew the next time I had to do something scary I would say to myself, "I dressed like a princess on an airplane. I can handle this."

Note: While I may be telling you this story in a humorous way, the experience completely opened my eyes to the courage that is shown every day by people who regularly go against what may be considered social or sexual "norms" in order to be true to themselves, especially when done amongst a peer group or family that is not supportive. That is true courage.

What's *your* Plane Princess?

This book isn't necessarily about getting you to jump out of planes, change careers, or try stand-up comedy (unless, of course, you want to). Being a Plane Princess for the day as outlined in the story above put me at the absolute outer edge of my Courage Zone with one foot in the Panic Zone. Your goal is simply to find out what puts *you* in that same spot. What is YOUR Plane Princess equivalent? For my volunteer, it was to get on Facebook. For others it might be to put up their hand in a meeting and say what they think. It could mean telling your parents you don't have time to visit them as often as they'd like. For a first grade girl it might mean telling that cute boy in class that she likes his shoes.

Exercise

What are some ways you can step out of your Comfort Zone in your personal life? Starting today!

You will move in and out of the zones

Let's talk about dating, which is a concept that excites and frightens most people. Especially a first date. Almost everyone on a first date is out of their Comfort Zone. How far out depends on you and maybe how good you think you look or whether or not that zit on your forehead has gone away. Let's say I'm out on a date and I'm feeling like I'm in the middle of my Courage Zone (after all, I REALLY dig this girl so I'm nervous). As the dinner progresses I say something that makes her laugh. That helps my confidence! I momentarily slide closer to my Comfort Zone. At the end of the night I ask for her phone number…and I get it! (Picture a happy dance here).

The next day I message her to say how much fun I had and maybe we can hang out again… but she doesn't reply. ALL DAY! The Inner Critic in my head starts saying things like "Hey loser, she gave you a fake number. She told all her friends about your stupid jokes. You're going to be single for life." In terms of this relationship I am now back in my

Courage Zone with the Panic Zone getting frighteningly close. I stress about it all day. Then I finally get a text from her explaining how she had dropped her phone in the sink and it was drying out in a bag of rice all day. "Sorry for taking so long to reply. Want to go out again?"

THANK GOD! I'm not a loser after all, she doesn't hate me and her friends aren't laughing at my Facebook pictures. I'm back in my Comfort Zone.

Starting a new job is the same. We so badly want to look competent and make a great first impression. In our first meeting we don't understand a word they're saying (many companies use a list of acronyms longer than the Great Wall of China). We're not feeling good. Then we make a comment, it's well received, and gosh darn it we're feeling more comfortable. That is, until we are assigned that project we've never done before and WHAM we're drifting towards the Panic Zone again.

Back and forth, back and forth. That is what a courageous life is all about.

But wait, my Comfort Zone is cozy

A very common question I get asked is "How do I know if I'm in my Comfort Zone too much, or just the right amount?" This is a great question because your Comfort Zone isn't a BAD place to be. Not at all. Sometimes it's exactly what you need. One of my favorite things to do in the world is to sit in front of the fireplace at my cottage reading a book. No courage involved there! I'm warm and toasty in my Comfort Zone and it feels fan-fricking-tastic, thank you very much. Some days, our Comfort Zone is exactly where we should be.

Not only is it cozy but it can also be *healthy*. There is no shortage of evidence that stress (which is fear in disguise, remember?) can wreak havoc on your health in the long-term. Stress attacks us in our Courage Zone and our Panic Zone.

Whether or not the time is right for you to step out of your Comfort Zone will often come down to a feeling. Remember that word, the f-word? The thing that is always trying to tell us something? Yeah, your feelings. We shouldn't put pressure on ourselves to constantly be out of our Comfort Zone, we should simply ask ourselves these questions:

- "Do I feel like I've been in my Comfort Zone too much lately?"
- "Am I happy with how much I've challenged myself lately?"
- "What would be the *opportunity* in stepping out of my Comfort Zone today/tomorrow/this week?"

Once you ask yourself those questions, you can often *feel* which answer is right for you. The right option may be scary, but inside you'll know if it's the right thing to do for the person you want to be, and the life you want to live.

Or you might answer them with a big fat "Yeah, I've been out of my Comfort Zone PLENTY lately. Gimme a bag of Doritos and watch me wedge myself between the couch cushions for the next 3 hours." That's fine too, so long as it feels like it's the right thing for you at that moment.

Mmmm, Doritos.

Courage versus Confidence

I am often asked "What's the difference between courage and confidence? Aren't they kind of the same?"

While they are not the same, they are very closely related. Imagine this scenario that I found myself in one day...

Story Time

My 89th skydive started out fine. I jumped with a friend and as we got stable in the air, falling at about 120 mph, we played a game of cat and mouse where one person chases the other. An experienced skydiver has so much control that they can literally fly in towards their partner, stop right in front of them, then turn around and fly off in the other direction.

At the end of our jump we separated and opened our parachutes. But mine didn't open all the way. It was maybe 75% open. It put me into a spin that I couldn't get out of. I would not survive if I landed in this spin. Thankfully, my training kicked in immediately. I checked my altitude to figure out how much time I had before I would need to deploy my reserve parachute. I looked at the lines (the ropes) and tried to open the rest of the parachute. It didn't work. I checked my altitude again, realizing I now had to open my reserve parachute. I knew that if my reserve didn't open, I would have about 13 seconds left to live. It was time to act.

I released the main parachute and opened my reserve. As it opened perfectly above me, my first thought was, "Hey... it's blue."

I'd never seen it before.

I felt surprisingly confident throughout the above life-and-death scenario because of two things. 1) I had the courage to act even though it was scary, and 2) Thanks to hours and hours of training, plus being familiar with skydiving statistics and the odds that my reserve would open, I was convinced that I would be alright. However, if that had been my FIRST skydive, I would have been terrified. I had so much less experience on my first jump and I wasn't as aware of the statistics and the odds.

Confidence = Courage + Expertise

The involvement of courage is clear: without the willingness to go into the unknown, face fears and try new things you will never be a truly confident person.

However, the more we can feel like an expert, the more confident we will feel. If I was asked to speak in front of 500 people on the topic of nuclear physics - which I know nothing about - part of me might be willing to try it (What a challenge! What a rush!) because I'm an expert speaker and a courageous person and I understand the opportunity in stepping out of my Comfort Zone. But since I am the farthest thing from an expert in nuclear physics, I would not feel *confident* going up there.

Similarly, someone with a PhD in nuclear physics might feel confident with the topic, but if they have never spoken in public before then they do not feel like an expert speaker. The only way to feel more confident is to become a more experienced speaker, and the only way to do that is to have the courage to try it.

You could stay in your present job for the rest of your life and be a very serious expert in it and therefore feel confident at work all the time, but without using and testing your courage you will not be a confident person in other areas of your life, not willing to try new things, not willing to grow and learn and live. And let's face it, nothing stays the same forever. Your job will change at some point or you could find yourself laid off when your company goes tits up. What will you do without courage then?

Let's look at Confidence in terms of our three circles:

Each time we step out of our Comfort Zone into our Courage Zone we experience fear, stress or some form of anxiety. Because of that, we never feel truly *confident* when we're being courageous because we don't feel like we know exactly what's happening or going to happen. However, each time we venture out there we know we are becoming a more courageous person overall, right? We also *learn* every time we're in our Courage Zone. It's impossible not to, because we're trying something new or different. Therefore every time we leap into that Courage Zone we are becoming slightly more of an expert on courage, and more of an expert on whatever the specific action is that we're undertaking.

Imagine you're on your way to an interview for a job you're extremely excited about. It matches your skills, your mission in life and the impact you wish to have, and gosh darn it seems like a super fun place to work. If it's a job that you're fully qualified for thanks to your experience, skills and education, then you will be confident going into it. However, Mother Nature and evolution will stop us from ever being a true expert in that one, most fearful area: not caring what others think of us. Therefore expertise alone will not get us there nor make us feel perfectly confident. We need courage as well.

We therefore feel the confidence AFTER we've been in the Courage Zone. We pushed past the fear and did it anyway. As a result we are a little bit more courageous and we increased our expertise.

This is also why being in your Comfort Zone sometimes is a good thing. Remember the Doritos? If we spent our whole life in the Courage Zone we would be a stress case. We would never feel like an expert and our confidence would start to erode.

Conclusions

Getting Clear On Increasing Courage

Courage is a muscle.

We grow it by exposure: stepping out of our
Comfort Zone in order to face fear.

Courage is relative. If something scares you, it counts
(regardless of what anyone else thinks).

Confidence = Courage + Expertise.

(RECESS!)

You've gotten through a big chunk of this book, so let's have recess.

Remember how excited you got for recess in school? It felt like the best part of the day - I would count the minutes while pretending to care what the teacher was talking about. How did we cram so much fun into 15 minutes?!

I found this definition of recess online: "the temporary withdrawal or cessation from the usual work or activity."

Borrrrrrrring.

This is my definition: "a short break to lighten up and have some silly fun."

I can't help it, I got the fun gene from my Mom. She's always ready to laugh, lighten up a situation or be silly. She's a breath of fresh air. My younger brother too - he's got a laugh that makes ME want to laugh.

So, how are we going to have a silly-fun recess right now? We're going to figure out what your stripper name is. That's right, your stripper name. Hypothetically speaking, of course.

Your first name is the name of your first pet. Your last name is the name of the first street you lived on. Therefore my stripper name is (drum-roll please)... Tigger Fontaine.

What's yours? Please share it with us on the Courage Crusade's Facebook page!

Yikes, the bell is ringing. Back to work!

ON YOU

"I can teach anybody how to get what they want out of life. The problem is that I can't find anybody who can tell me what they want."
Mark Twain

Take a deep, deep breath. We have covered some big hairy stuff so far and you're still here. I'm really proud of you.

Now that we're clear on courage and fear, it's time to get more clear on YOU. Yes, you. After all, this book is a complete waste of your time if it doesn't help you become more of the person you want to be. The kind of person who feels like bounding out their front door every morning with arms spread wide, yelling to the world, "Are you ready?!"

If you're not much of a yell-at-your-neighborhood kind of person, no problem, you can just whisper it. As long as you FEEL it.

Most people I talk to understand pretty quickly the importance of "living a life that's true to myself". They can see the benefit of that. Sometimes what's holding them back from doing it is covered in the previous pages: they don't understand that fear can be used to our advantage and that courageous living is within our grasp.

But even more common is to hear someone say in a fit of frustration, "But how do I figure out what I *want*?! What if I don't have a clue what 'living true to myself' looks like, because I don't really know myself?"

There are countless books telling you to be yourself, follow your passion, carve your path, blah blah blah…. But most fail miserably at telling you *how to figure out that part*. This is where we start that process. While I can't tell you who you are, I can show you how to figure it out for yourself.

Without that knowledge you will always be stuck in the bottom area of the graph:

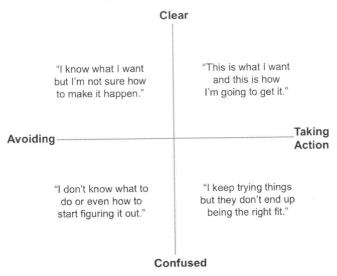

I don't know what to do or even how to start figuring it out.
or
I keep trying things but they don't end up being the right fit.

Why is it so daunting to figure *you* out?

We touched on this earlier but it is crucial to understand, so let's dig deeper.

The reason most people don't bother to figure out this self-awareness stuff is because they're scared of what they might figure out. What if what you have (career, spouse, friends, field of study, hobby) doesn't fit who you are and what you want? That means something needs to change, and as we've already discussed, we are programmed to fear change and avoid it at all costs.

And what if changing to get a better fit means you upset the people in your life? What if you have to disappoint someone? What will they think of you?

There is another reason why self-awareness is scary for many people: "What if I realize I'm not good at anything"? I have seen countless clients who were struggling with that exact thought.

But I'll tell you where you can shove that question right now, because EVERYone is good at something. Everyone. Say it with me now, "I am amazing at something." It took me a long time to fully accept that I'm amazing at things, but that's when our life really blossoms.

Remember what we said about "fit". We want a job that allows us to use our strengths (our amazingness) and focus our 9-5 on something that is important to us. We want friends and a partner/spouse with similar values and interests. We want a neighborhood that has the services we need and makes us feel comfortable. We want a car that fits our needs - station wagon for the dog, or pick-up truck for the snowmobile. Fit fit fit. Just like a pair of pants that is too tight, you can try to ignore the bad fits in your life but you always know they're there. So let's pull that underwear out of our ass and get a better fit.

Every single one of us is unique. When you hide the true you, you inevitably end up being like everyone else. And there is already enough people in the world trying to be like everyone else! In fact, you are doing OTHER people a disservice by not being you, because you're adding to the polluted pool of conformity and depriving us of experiencing your uniqueness. Boo!

In the words of the best author ever, Dr Seuss, "Be who you are and say what you feel, because those who mind don't matter, and those who matter don't mind."

I'm a courage expert but I *still* struggle sometimes with what other people will think of the real me and the life I choose. But I do my absolute best. When I get changed in the gym locker room and I'm standing there in nothing but my Superman underwear, I say to myself "It doesn't matter what they think, it doesn't matter what they think." When my hockey buddies order a pitcher of beer, I proudly order myself a fruity girly drink because, gosh darn it, I like 'em! And...AND (are you ready for this?), I sit down to pee! Every time! And I'm a man!

Let's snoop around your home

When we were little kids we were excited to show our friends our bedroom. "Hey, wanna see my room?!" Your room expressed who you were and what you aspired to be. I had pictures of athletes and superheroes. My room represented what excited me about life.

As an adult, does your room (or apartment/condo/house) reflect who you are? Or is it "safe"? Are your dreams and style dictated by Pottery Barn because someone decided that's how adults should act? Could a stranger walk into your place, look around, and get a feel for who you really are as an individual? Or does it look like everyone else's place? Have all the bright colors, stripes and polka dots of your sunny childhood been replaced by the solid colors of don't-rock-the-boat adulthood?

Don't get me wrong, I have experienced a mild stirring in my loins when I'm in Pottery Barn (some of that stuff is sweet!), but I make sure to add my own touch of Billy. My bedroom is bright green with a canoe paddle on the wall, a picture of Muhammad Ali, and a huge quote that says "If at first you don't succeed, skydiving is not for you." My room is 100% me.

So look around your home. Does it reflect you? Does it show what your priorities are? Your hopes and dreams? If it does, then good for you – you have the guts to stand up for who you want to be. If it doesn't, what's holding you back? What do you need to let go of in order to let the real you shine through?

A young person is someone who has more dreams for the future than memories. So, be young.

Exercise

How does YOUR uniqueness show up? Does your home show the real you? If you asked your friends "How am I unique?" what would they say? Try asking them!

What do you value?

In terms of being true to you, there is nothing more important than knowing what your Values are and how to apply them. Absolutely nothing.

How does knowing your Values help you in your life?
- Making better decisions, especially when they seem really hard.
- Dealing with difficult relationships.
- Handling your emotions and not letting them get the best of you.
- Understanding why you're in a crappy (or amazing) mood.
- Figuring out which relationships are worth keeping and which need to end.
- Picking your next job or career.

And the list goes on and on!

Every single emotion you feel is connected to your Values. When someone insults you and you want to scream or insult them back, it's because they've stepped on one or more of your Values. When you accomplish something incredibly important to you and you're so happy and proud you could cry - it's because you've lived true to one or more of your Values.

The all-knowing, all-powerful Google defines a Value as follows:
> "A person's principles or standards of behavior; one's judgment of what is important in life."

Values are the things you need to have in your life to ensure you are as fulfilled as you can possibly be and to ensure you are performing at your absolute best.

Once you know your Values you can look at any good or bad experience in your life and know exactly why it felt that way. Then you can get more of the good stuff in your life, and less of the stuff that makes you unhappy.

Enough talk! Let's get down to business and identify YOUR Values.

On the next page is a list of Values. It is not exhaustive, but it's a good start. Begin by highlighting or underlining *all* the values in the list that resonate with you. Choose as many as you want.

Accomplishment	Freedom	Privacy
Success	Friendship	Progress
Accountability	Fun	Prosperity, Wealth
Accuracy	Global view	Punctuality
Adventure	Good will	Quality of work
Beauty	Goodness	Reliability
Calm, peace	Gratitude	Resourcefulness
Challenge	Hard work	Respect for others
Change	Harmony	Responsiveness
Cleanliness,	Honesty	Results-oriented
orderliness	Humility	Safety
Commitment	Improvement	Satisfying others
Communication	Independence	Security
Community	Individuality	Self-givingness
Competence	Inner peace, calm	Self-reliance
Competition	Innovation	Self-thinking
Concern for others	Integrity	Service (to others)
Connection	Intensity	Simplicity
Continual	Justice	Skill
improvement	Knowledge	Solving Problems
Cooperation	Leadership	Speed
Coordination	Love, Romance	Stability
Creativity	Loyalty	Standardization
Customer	Maximum	Status
satisfaction	utilization	Strength
Decisiveness	(of time, resources)	A will to succeed
Delight of being, joy	Meaning	Systemization
Democracy	Money	Teamwork
Discipline	Openness	Timeliness
Discovery	Patriotism	Tolerance
Diversity	Peace, Non-	Tradition
Efficiency	violence	Tranquility
Equality	Perfection	Trust
Excellence	Personal Growth	Truth
Fairness	Pleasure	Unity
Faith	Power	Variety
Faithfulness	Practicality	Wisdom
Family	Preservation	
Flair		

Like most people, you probably highlighted a whole bunch! That's totally fine - I did that too the first time. Now you will answer some value-based questions in order to shine further light on the Values in that list that are MOST important to you. After all, we need to narrow your big list down to your top 10.

1. What are 3 peak moments in your life? Moments when you were happiest, most satisfied, or felt like you were truly "kicking ass".

   _____

   _____

   _____

2. When were you most proud of yourself? (list 2 or 3).

   _____

   _____

   _____

3. What are two low moments / two least proud moments?

   _____

   _____

   _____

4. Who are 2 or 3 people that you really admire, respect or look up to? Why?

   _____

_____

_____

After you answer those questions, you're going to narrow down your Values list to your Top 10 and put them *in order of priority* with 1 being the most important. As you do so, keep in mind your answers to the above questions because they will shine light on what is most important to you.

Don't try to rationalize which Values make your top 10 list, just go instead with what feels best for you. Don't think about your job or your personal life specifically, or the Values you feel you SHOULD have. Just think about YOU and what feels important and what energizes you! If narrowing that list down to 10 isn't easy, don't worry! It's hard for everyone.

1. _____

2. _____

3. _____

4. _____

5. _____

6. _____

7. _____

8. _____

9. _____

10. _____

So that's it? These are my Values for Life?

Nope. These are your Values for *now*. Some may never change, but some might. As you start becoming more aware of your Values going forward, you may find that some are not as important as you thought. Or you may realize something is missing.

But what do they *really* mean?

Now you have a list of your top 10 Values. Congratulations! Most people will never reach this level of self-awareness. Yah, seriously, never. You're becoming a Jedi Knight of your life.

"Luke, I am your father."

Now you are going to define each of your Values in your own words. We do this because even though our Values may be words that we use regularly and we may be speaking the same language as the people in our life, we each have slightly different ideas of what words mean. This is compounded greatly when it comes to our Values because they are things we feel very strongly about. And the higher up your list a Value sits, the more of a specific meaning you will apply to that word.

For example, some people have "Respect" as one of their Values. For them, Respect might mean always being punctual and following through on their word. For someone else, Respect could mean treating other people well and not talking down to anyone.

Defining each of your Values will help you understand them better as well as see whether or not they overlap.

Exercise

Define each of your Values in your own words.

Did any of your Values change after defining them? Did you find a different word that describes a Value even better than the word in the list? Or perhaps you found two values were quite similar and could possibly be combined?

Each of your Values should really resonate with you because they are unique to you. I believe in sharing, so here is my Values list:

Freedom, Community, Fun, Honesty/Respect, Productivity, Value to others, Adventure, Discovery, Simplicity, Rocking the boat

You get to decide what your Values mean for you. I don't have Family or Friends or Love in my Values because I consider them all to fit under the single value of Community. If you have the word Community as a value but you prefer a different word for that (such as Tribe or Crew) go ahead and use it, even if it's not on the list. The list is just to get you thinking, but you can use any other words you like. My 10th Value is "Rocking the boat" which isn't on the list, but over time I've come to realize it's something that's very important to me, so I put it in.

When you read through your list of 10 Values you should feel energized! It's who you are as a person, at the core! They are the things that are most important to you and they make you who you are.

Where's the proof?

Okay, how about some proof that those Values of yours are really as impactful as I'm saying. Sound good? Go back to the Values questions: peak moments of your life, low moments and people you look up to.

Pick one of them and then see which of your Values were affected in that scenario. If you're looking at a peak moment, you can identify which of your Values you were honoring in that moment. It's probably a few. For a low moment in your life you'll be able to identify which Values you were NOT honoring. Or sometimes it has nothing to do with you and it's someone else who was stepping on some of your Values.

The people you look up to are people who exemplify some of your Values. If you *really* look up to someone, they probably exemplify many of your values.

One of my peak moments in life was when I sang a song that I wrote and played guitar to a group of about 70 people. I was sweating buckets I was so nervous. It was a feel-good song, all about the audience, and it got a standing ovation. I still get goose-bumps just thinking about it! So, which Values of mine was I honoring in that scenario? Freedom, Community, Fun, Adventure, and Value to Others. No wonder it felt so good.

Conversely, one of my least proud moments in my life was when I was in an argument with a friend in university, and I said some VERY hurtful things to him. I didn't actually believe what I said, I just said it because I knew it would get under his skin. It was a terrible thing to do, I know! I still feel bad about it. How is that related to my Values? I was totally stepping on my Values of Community, Honesty/Respect, Value to Others. Pounding them into the ground. No wonder it's a low moment for me.

Our best or worst moments in life will affect many of our Values at the same time, and often one or more in the top 3.

You're a human being

One of the great things about Values is they allow you to focus on who you're BEING. We spend so much time focusing on what we're DOING or what has to 'get done' but we are human beings, not human doings. Anything we aim to do has some degree of uncertainty to it because other factors will be involved. You may want to address an issue with a family member, but how they react isn't completely in your control. But who you choose to BE during the discussion is completely in your control.

Your impact

Some people look at all this Values talk and say "But it seems a bit selfish to focus totally on me all the time. You're asking me to focus on myself (my Values). Seems a bit self-centred. What about everyone else?"

It's a brilliant question. In order to answer it, take a look at your Values. Go through your Values and identify which Values, if honored, will benefit other people. The truth is, you can NOT honor all your Values without having a positive impact on others. I'll go through my Values as an example:

1. Freedom - this is one of my Values that is actually mostly about me. Doesn't really benefit others.

2. Community - this is ALL about other people. I honour this Value by treating my community (friends, family...) well.

3. Fun - sometimes this is a solo thing, but more often it involves adding fun to other people's lives.

4. Honesty/Respect - this is all about others. Being respectful and honest to people makes their life better too.

5. Productivity - mostly about me.

6. Discovery - this is often about others because it causes me to show interest in people and then they feel heard and understood.

7. Value to Others - this is obvious! All about other people.

93

8. Adventure - sometimes just me, sometimes includes others.

9. Simplicity - all me.

10. Rocking the Boat - all me.

As you can see, I can't live true to many of those Values (especially 2, 3, 4, 7) without other people benefitting directly. In other words, when you live true to your Values not only are YOU more fulfilled in life, but other people will be as well. Everybody wins.

Unhappy Values

The unhappy list you created at the beginning of this book was a great start. Many people will never do that even once in their life. But knowing what you're unhappy about doesn't necessarily mean you know how to make it any better.

Your Values help explain *why* those things are making you unhappy. They explain what is lacking or being challenged.

Exercise

Go back to your unhappy list. For each of the items on your list, which of your Values are not being honored?

Do you now see why you're not satisfied with those things on your list?

In the last full-time job I had before starting my own business, I wasn't happy. I wasn't sure what the problem was but I just wasn't feeling motivated or fulfilled. I could have looked at my Values at the time (if I had known them then!)

and I would have seen which Values were not being honored in that job. They would have been my Values of Adventure, Discovery, Simplicity, and Rocking-the-boat. Those were all the things I didn't feel I was getting in that job. Those are all very important to me, so no wonder I wasn't happy.

Go to bed with your Values

1. Read your Values once every single day for a month
From now on, read your list of 10 Values once every day. In doing this you will start to notice how they show up in your life. Remember, any strong emotion you feel is related to Values, so identify which one(s) it is in the moment. Every time you feel an emotion (either good or bad) look through your list and see which Values are involved.

I find the best time of day to do this is before I go to bed when the activities of the day are fresh in my mind. Fresh emotions are always the most powerful. Remember the "f" word? Feelings? Feelings are your emotions and therefore they reflect your Values.

- Which Values did I honor today?
- Which Values did I neglect? (This is ok, by the way. We can't honor all of them every day)
- Which Values do I feel are lacking lately?
- Which Values were stepped on by other people?

What are you great at?

As I sit here in my cottage in the woods, writing this chapter, the Olympics are only a couple of weeks away. It got me thinking. Those gold-winning athletes are the best in the WORLD at something on that day. In the world! 7 billion people live on this big rock floating in space, but on that day those Olympians are the best. That's amazing to me. So then I started thinking… what could I be the best in the world at? Imagine you had 4 years to become the best in the world at something. What would it be?

My first thoughts were existing Olympic events, but there aren't too many old-man Olympic sports other than curling, and to be honest I'd rather pound my tongue flat with a frozen leg of lamb than be a curler. No offence, curlers, I respect the game and you're very talented, it just doesn't fit what I enjoy.

So what else could I do? Well, I first narrowed it down to things where I had an immediate advantage. For example, if I spent the next 4 years practicing, I bet I could be the best snowball-maker in the world. After all, how many billions of people don't even have access to snow? I'd beat them for sure.

The fact is, it is more fun to do things you're good at. Not all the time (remember comfort zones) but as a career it sure feels good to know what you're doing a bunch of the time.

We all have things that we're amazing at. The problem is, we very often aren't aware of them. This is especially true with natural talents we've had since birth, such as great communication skills, empathy (reading people's feelings), leading others. We take our natural gifts for granted because we've always been good at them. Therefore they don't feel special and we assume *everyone* must be great at them.

If you take those gifts for granted, you're probably not leveraging them as best you can. Imagine a life that had you living true to your Values, using your strengths every day, and not having to use your weaknesses? That sounds pretty damn sweet to me.

While I believe in constant improvement, I also believe in leveraging what comes naturally. We all like to be good! That's when we gain confidence.

In a typical performance review in a job, you are given a brief pat on the back for what you did well in the last year then the boss goes into detail about all the things you need to get better at. While it's crucial in life to continually strive for improvement, if you don't ENJOY the task they're telling you to get better at, you shouldn't have to do it! Most companies are full of people doing stuff they don't like to do. How effective can you be at something when you don't like it? Not very damn effective. Sometimes we just need to improve our proficiency at something to start enjoying it more, but I believe if the activity doesn't inspire SOME sense of interest or passion in you, it's probably not worth focusing on.

A perfect set-up at work would consist of people who love what they do and compensate for each other's weaknesses. If I need to hire a partner for a project, I want someone who shares the PASSION for the project (which will relate to our Values) but I want him or her to be great at all the things I suck at and don't enjoy doing!

I actually believe the terms "strengths" and "weaknesses" are misleading. The things we are good at and enjoy will *energize* us when we do them. The things we're not good at or don't enjoy will *drain* us. And when we feel drained, we don't do our best work. And we're miserable. That's when we procrastinate.

But sometimes it makes sense to improve a skill we're not great at. Think of a professional tennis player who has a fantastic shot in every way except her backhand. Her backhand sucks. It's a weakness. Should she ignore it and focus on her other shots? If she does that she's never going to make it very far. In this case she does need to improve that weakness, but she's not doing it simply because it's a weakness, she's doing it because it aligns with her bigger goal - becoming the best tennis player she can be. Unless she perfects the backhand, she will never reach her true potential in the game she loves. While she's not yet good at the backhand, the thought of getting better at it probably *energizes* her.

There's a difference between hating something because you're not good at it, and hating something because it just doesn't excite you. The first few times Roger Federer swung a tennis racket, he probably wasn't very good at it. But I bet it sparked something in him. I bet it energized him. That would give him the drive to become better at it.

I'm a motivational speaker and the first time I spoke in front of a large group, I wasn't very good. But it energized the hell out of me. It excited me. It honored a whole bunch of my Values. So I kept working at it.

In my own business I hate accounting. It has to get done in order for me to have a successfully functioning business, but I have absolutely no interest in it. It drains me rather than energizes me. That means I should hire someone else to do it so I can focus on what energizes me. I put it through what I call the 'improve or outsource filter': can I become the best courage expert in the world without knowing accounting? Yep. So then I don't need to get better at it. I can outsource it to someone else.

So, let's strike the terms "strengths" and "weaknesses" from our vocabulary and replace them instead with "energizers" and "drainers."

Your life should be set up so that, ideally, you only have to use your energizers. Otherwise...

> If you focus on improving the things that drain you, you won't get past mediocrity.

If you aren't sure what your energizers are, you're not alone. Very few of my clients have an accurate idea of this when we start.

Alright, enough chit chat. Let's figure out YOUR energizers.

Strengths (Energizers) Assessment

There is no shortage of strengths tests out there for you to try. Most of them can provide you with some insight but I believe that all assessments are simply great conversation starters. Assessment results will vary greatly depending on the mood you're in when you do it. If an assessment asks you to rate your present level of self-confidence but you just got fired from your job yesterday and dumped by your spouse, you'll rate it lower than you did last month when you were kicking ass in your life.

The real value of assessments is in the playback when a qualified person goes through the results with you and gets you to dig deeper. Having said that, doing an assessment without that playback is way better than not doing one at all.

So, I'd like you to complete this world-renowned assessment that I do with all my clients. There is no cost for the basic results. It will give you a list of your "character" strengths. The assessment uses the same 24 character strengths for everyone, but it will put yours in order.

Do the VIA survey at: **www.viacharacter.org**

After completing the assessment you can click on the "Free Report", or feel free to pay for the more detailed report if you wish. We will focus on your top 5 (which I call your "Energizers") and your bottom 5 (your "Drainers"). Here are mine:

- <u>Energizers</u>: Humor, Curiosity, Honesty, Judgment, Bravery
- <u>Drainers</u>: Prudence, Self-regulation, Perseverance, Forgiveness, Humility

When I'm going into a new client meeting that I'm anxious about, I look at my Energizers to see what I can leverage. I can use "Humor" by starting the meeting with a light joke or a fun game, and I can always use "Curiosity" by asking lots of questions to get to the root of their challenges. Both of those make me more energized - and therefore a bit less anxious - about the meeting.

Remember, you can always improve your Drainers, but it probably won't be very enjoyable to do so. So focus on what comes naturally. Ideally, we want to set up our lives so that we are living true to our Values, we have lots of opportunities to use our Energizers, and not a lot of need to use our Drainers.

Really? I'm not good at THAT?

After doing the VIA assessment, my clients look at their top 5 (the Energizers) and say, "Yeah, that seems pretty accurate." But when they see their Drainers they often say, "Hang on a second, I'm actually pretty good at that one. This is wrong!"

We don't like admitting we may not be great at something.

"What will people think if I'm not good at this?" If you find yourself surprised at your Drainers, make sure you read their full definition from the survey. Sometimes they may define an item slightly different than you do. Sure you may be good at them if you really have to, but they don't energize you.

Note: in this assessment, all the definitions are written as if they were true for you (in other words, as if they were Energizers). However, if it appears at the bottom of your list, it means the definition is NOT true for you. For example, at the very bottom of my list is Humility which says, "You do not seek the spotlight, preferring to let your accomplishments speak for themselves. You do not regard yourself as special, and others recognize and value your modesty."

Since it is a Drainer and therefore at the bottom of my list, it means it is NOT true for me. It actually means I do seek the spotlight and I do regard myself as special...." Keep this in mind as you look through the definitions.

Exercise

Look at your unhappy list. How could you use your Energizers to improve that list? What about your Drainers - do you need to rely on them often in your present situation? If so, that won't feel great and it won't be much fun either. How can you compensate for your Drainers by focusing more on using your Energizers?

What is your Life Purpose?

Most organizations (corporations, non-profits, schools...) have a Mission and/or Vision Statement, as well as Values or "pillars." The purpose of these is to provide them with an identity; defining who they are and what they stand for. It is their WHY, answering the question "Why do we exist?"

This is their version of being "Clear."

It helps them make strategic decisions. Every decision an organization makes should fit its Mission and Values. Many companies start to falter when they have what is called "Mission Drift" where they stray from their Mission - often in pursuit of money - and lose their identity.

That's because so many organizations and people focus way too much on WHAT they do, not WHY they do it. There is a great TED talk about this exact topic by the Why guru himself, Simon Sinek.

People function the same as organizations. If you don't know what your Mission Statement is, how do you know what to do every day? What are you striving for? When you're faced with a big decision, how do you decide? With your gut? Our gut can add value, no question about it, but our gut usually tells us to do what's safe and has the least chance of making us fail or look silly. The Values you figured out earlier in this book are the first step to better decision-making, while knowing your mission statement adds even more clarity.

The term "Mission Statement" sounds way too formal and corporate to me, so I call it "Life Purpose" instead. Your Life Purpose is the way you're going to put your Values into *action*. It is the impact you want to have.

To be perfectly honest, it's difficult to accurately define your very own Life Purpose just by reading a book. This book can *help*, but some form of live discussion is often required to make it perfectly tailored to you as an individual. While I do offer live coaching on this topic (yes, this is me shamelessly self-promoting my services) you can definitely get started figuring out your Life Purpose here. I'll do my best to guide you from the pages of this book. The first step is to write your Eulogy.

Excuse me?

Yes, your Eulogy. The nice stuff that someone would say about you at your funeral. Sounds kind of sick, doesn't it? But think about it; at a funeral, people talk about all the fantastic things the person did or stood for in their life. It's always positive.

Years ago I was sitting at my friend's dad's funeral. A very funny, top-quality guy who died too young. Different people went up to the front and spoke about how much they loved Fred, how much they would miss him, how unique and amazing he was. I sat there thinking to myself, "Did he ever hear this stuff?! It would feel so good!"

Our funeral is often the only guaranteed time in our life that people will tell us all the great things they think about us. AND WE'RE NOT ABLE TO HEAR IT! What a shame.

A eulogy isn't about inside jokes and funny stories, it's about the *impact* you had on others. "Andre had a great laugh that made you want to laugh too" or "Chris would do anything for you when you needed help". Your Eulogy will help you see how you want to be remembered, pulling out all the qualities you most value in yourself and summarizing who you want to be in the world.

Writing it isn't as terrifying an exercise as it may sound. Most of the people I've worked with have procrastinated writing their eulogy until the very last day before they had to send it to me, but once they started doing it they said it wasn't as bad as they expected. And it can teach you a LOT about who you are and what makes you tick.

Exercise (this one is really important and will be VERY helpful to you)

Write your Eulogy. All the nice things that you'd like to hear someone say about you at your funeral. What you were loved for, what impact you had, how you will be remembered.

Note: if you're really struggling to write your Eulogy, take a break and then try again. Just start writing *something*. If you simply can't seem to get going, send the questions below to 3 or 4 people you are closest to; people who know you well and whose opinion you respect.

- What am I really good at?
- If I was a car, what kind would I be?
- How do I make people feel when they're with me?
- If I was no longer in your life, you would most miss…(complete the sentence)
- You think I could be an even happier person if I… (complete the sentence)

Their answers will help you get the ball rolling.

Did you write your Eulogy? If so, nicely done! How did it feel? Was it scary at first? It was when I did it, that's for damn sure.

If you did NOT write it yet, then you're giving power to your fear. You'll be happier and feel more empowered if you write it. Just saying. ☺

Now we take your Eulogy and transform it into the first draft of your Life Purpose. Don't worry, it's just a first draft, you can revise it as many times as you like. It's important to get something down on paper even if it changes completely later on.

Defining Your Life Purpose

The good news is that ANY Life Purpose can be great so long as YOU think it's great. As long as it energizes you when you read it and it makes you proud to be you. There are a few guidelines to follow to ensure it is as fitting as possible.

Read your Eulogy and see what stands out. What makes you most proud? What parts *feel* the best? What patterns do you see?

Write a one sentence Life Purpose based on your Eulogy. Your Life Purpose is an action statement that sums up what you stand for and/or what your impact is on others. It's based on what you're naturally good at and what means the most to you. Here are a few examples:

"I give people the courage to be who they're meant to be."
"Helping people excel along new paths."
"I help others bounce back from difficult relationships."
"Supporting others in achieving their goals."

You'll notice in the above examples that a Life Purpose is written in terms of its impact on others. This is how we add the most value and therefore belong and therefore feel super crazy awesome about life and our place in it. If your first draft of your Life Purpose is just about YOU, then ask yourself, "If I do that really well, what value does it add for other people?"

For example, one of my client's first draft of her Life Purpose was "To be a great leader." Then I asked her "If you're being a great leader, what is the impact on others?" She replied "I help them get out of a jam." That became her Life Purpose: "Help others get out of a jam."

Your Life Purpose is your Values in action

Take a look at your Values. If you're living true to your Life Purpose, which of your Values are you fulfilling? Probably lots of them. Your Values can give you different ideas as to how to live your Life Purpose at any given time. If I'm feeling low in my Adventure Value, then I ask myself "How can I live true to my Life Purpose in an *adventurous* way this week?" Another week I may feel like my Community Value is a bit low. How can I live true to my Life Purpose with respect to my Community?

The final Life Purpose test...

Can you live true to your Life Purpose if you're thrown in jail? You need to be able to. This ensures that your Life Purpose is 100% within your control to execute.

For example, one of my client's first draft of her Life Purpose was "To give my children the best life possible." But what if her kids decide one day they don't want her help? What if - god forbid - they pass away? Your Life Purpose can't rely on any specific people because then it's not in your control. She revised her Life Purpose to be "Helping people excel along new paths." I can't imagine a better definition of parenting than that!

Would she be able to live true to that purpose in jail? Yep. It passes the jail test.

She can choose to *apply* her Life Purpose to her kids more than anyone else, but writing it more generically means she can also apply it elsewhere, such as in her job. And what makes a better leader than "helping others excel along new paths"?

This rocked my world

I'll share a pattern with you that I've been noticing. I now believe that your ultimate Life Purpose is to help others who are struggling with the biggest struggle that YOU went through in your life.

I've had lots of struggles but my biggest one was being 100% myself and living a life that was right for me, not for everyone else. I worried so much what other people thought. It impacted my career choices, friends, the clothes I wore, everything! And coincidently, this is exactly what I now dedicate my life to.

Does this theory relate to the Life Purpose you came up with? Does your Life Purpose relate in some way to a big struggle you experienced in your life? If not, don't worry, everyone is unique and this is just your first draft. We are talking about some seriously heavy shit here, so you can digest it for a while and come back to it later. I've been tweaking my Life Purpose for years, so give yourself some time.

Work vs Life

Some people feel they can live their Life Purpose at home but not at work, or vice versa, with friends but not some family members. But the truth is, you are ONE person. You are not someone different when you walk into your job versus when you're at home on your couch. You may ACT a little different at work, but you are still the same individual. Adults are simply big kids who are able to wear different hats at different times. When all the areas of your life (including your job) are the right fit for you as an individual, you won't have to wear so many different hats. When your job is a perfect fit for you, you can be 100% yourself.

So once you know your Life Purpose, being the best version of yourself includes having the courage to live true to it in every single area of your life.

Now what?

Now that you have the first draft of your Life Purpose, sit with it for a while. I recommend you read your Life Purpose, Values, Energizers and Drainers once a day. Then you will start to notice how they all show up in your life. Remember to watch for moments when you feel a strong emotion like anger, hurt, happiness or fulfillment. How did your Life Purpose fit into that (or not)?

Life Purpose reminders

- It's written in terms of your impact on others.
- It's an action statement starting with a verb.
- It's generic enough that it doesn't apply only to specific people in your life.
- You can live true to your Life Purpose even if you're sent to jail.

If you're *still* struggling with defining your Life Purpose, try using this formula: I help X with Y so that Z. Such as "I help (young people) be more (courageous) so they can (get a life that excites the hell out of them)."

So, are you cool?

Now that you have a better idea of who you are as an individual and what makes you tick, let's talk about whether or not you're "cool."

I hate that word. It comes with so many stereotypes. Cool looks like this or acts like that, or drives this or makes that much money. As soon as we use the word "cool" - or any other adjective or adverb for that matter - we are making a judgment. That means it is impacted by our own fears and filters.

When I switched high schools after grade nine I was obsessed with being "cool." I wanted to fit in. Being cool meant other people might like me and then I'd belong. Cool was popular. Cool dressed like a winner. If you were cool you had friends. Cool guys got the hot girls. But then why do some of those people from high school who were considered cool at the time actually seem like total douche-bags to me when I think back on them now?

Sorry, that was an unfair judgment. They weren't douche-bags, they were just...different. Like, annoying-as-hell different.

Years later I changed my definition of cool. In my not-so-humble opinion, YOU are cool if two things are true:
- You have the guts to be 100% yourself
- You treat people well

That's it. You get bonus points if you strive to make the world a better place :)

Doesn't matter to me how much money you make, what you

drive, who you hang out with, what your hobbies are, how fit your butt is... if you're being yourself and you treat people well, I think you're cool.

But my opinion of you *does not matter*. As long as YOU like yourself, my opinion means diddly squat. We all get to invent our own definition of cool, because we get to decide who we are going to be.

This is great news. It means I can still be cool if I end up doing not-so-cool things. Here are a few not-so-cool things that happen to me:

- Strolling out of a public washroom with a piece of toilet paper stuck to the bottom of my shoe.
- Missing a belt loop at the back of my pants. I could be Brad Pitt wearing an Armani suit while winning an Oscar but if I miss a belt loop I feel like a total chump.
- A piece of lettuce stuck in my teeth? Yep, happens regularly. In fact I probably have one right now.
- One day while riding my brand new mountain bike, feeling like "the man," when from out of nowhere came a sneeze that would make a hurricane look like a light breeze. I sneezed ALL OVER myself and almost fell off my bike.

Those are definitely not considered "cool" moments. But let's all breathe a big sigh of relief because each of us gets to decide what cool is. While those embarrassing moments may (will) happen again, I know who I am, what I stand for, and the positive impact I'm having on the world. A mouthful of teeth-lettuce can't change that.

So that's me, now what?

"You are Braver than you believe, Smarter than you seem, and Stronger than you think."
Winnie the Pooh

The unhappy list you created at the beginning of this book was a great start, but knowing what you're unhappy about doesn't necessarily mean you know how to make it better.

We need to transform those unhappy things into *changes* you want to see in your life. Luckily you now have a better idea what's important to you and what you're good at, so you can see exactly WHY those things don't fit with who you are and who you want to be.

Exercise

Go back to your unhappy list to see why those things don't *fit* you. For each item on your list...

a) Compare it against your Values. Which Values are not being honored?

b) Compare against your Energizers and Drainers. Does it allow you to use your Energizers and not have to rely on your Drainers?

c) Compare against your Life Purpose (even if it's still just a work in progress). Does it fit?

Do you now see why you're not satisfied with those things on your list? Once this is done, we can start to be proactive, identifying specific *changes* you want in your life. Then we can start to take action to make those changes a reality and get a better fit.

Exercise

For each item on your unhappy list, ask yourself these questions in order to transform them into changes...

a) What exactly do you want to be different about it? How would it look if your Values, Life Purpose and Energizers were being honored better?

b) What is in your control to make this change? What isn't?

c) What's the first step in making this happen? What can you start doing today?

That question about control is important because we should only ever focus on what is in our control or we will feel supremely helpless and disempowered. This often happens with money. We may be unhappy with how much money we're earning but that's not easy to change overnight. We have to define the first steps in earning more money. Maybe we need to change jobs, or take a course or go back to school, or find something that allows us to use our Energizers more often and therefore add more value. Or perhaps we need to let go of other things in our life (too many hobbies, unnecessary spending) to make more time for earning.

Write each item on your list as a change that can be acted on. Here are some that could apply to me right now:

Unhappy list
1. Life feels kind of dull lately
2. I'm not talking to one of my old friends
3. Not enough disposable income

Why doesn't it fit me? What's lacking?
1. Values: Adventure, Fun, Freedom, Rocking the Boat. Energizers: Humor, Bravery.

2. Values: Community, Honesty/Respect, Fun.
   Drainers: Forgiveness (since this doesn't come naturally to me, it drains me when I have to forgive).
3. Values: Freedom, Fun, Value to Others.
   Life Purpose: I will be better able to "Inspire people to be who they're meant to be" if I have more resources.

What do I want to change?
1. I want adventure and fun. To do this I could start conversations with more strangers, start a new hobby, or allow myself to be more silly.
2. I want to know I made an effort to repair our friendship. I could let go of my own desire to be right, reach out to him, explain my point of view, see how he feels and whether we're still a good fit as friends.
3. To get more disposable income I will re-look at my budgeting and see where I can cut unnecessary spending.

Want some cheese with that whine?

Now we have a list of changes we want in our life and we no longer have an excuse to whine about what we're unhappy with. You know those people? They just bitch and complain non-stop but they don't choose to do anything about it. Their unhappiness is always the fault of someone or something else.

Sometimes life hands us very difficult, unfair things to deal with. No doubt about it. I sometimes hear stories from my clients that make me want to cry. But we always have two options: accept it as it is, or try to change/improve it. Either way, stop complaining. It makes the complainer feel disempowered and it brings down the people you're talking to.

There is nothing wrong with *proactive* complaining; stating what you're unhappy with in order to understand it better so you can figure out what to do about it. Sometimes we want to share our troubles with others in order to feel support and get help. Of course we do, we're social creatures. But try to catch yourself if it starts to drag on without any improvement. You're not doing anyone any good, including yourself.

One of my former clients was a parent who suffered a horrible loss. We were both crying on the phone during the coaching call and I still think about her regularly. She wasn't whining or complaining to me though. She felt stuck and she was looking for support and a way to move forward because what she had tried so far was not working. She was strong as a bull and she worked hard to improve the situation.

The Perfect Life

I'm excited to now share with you my definition of the Perfect Life. It's within your reach, but it may not be quite what you expected.

We've talked a bunch about control. We feel most empowered when we feel in control of our life. That's why it's so important to ask yourself "What's in my control here?" when you have a goal or a change you're working on. With that in mind, this is my definition of perfection in every single area of your life:

- You live true to your Values consistently.
- You deliver on your Life Purpose in everything you do.
- You have ample opportunities to use your Energizers.
- You're not often required to use your Drainers.
- You step out of your comfort zone often.

That's it. Those are the things that are completely in your control every single day. Add in a whole bunch of fun and laughter and you're doing everything you can to ensure a smile on your face and a deep sense of meaning in your life every damn day. That's as perfect as life gets. And it's within your control.

Conclusions

Getting Clear On Increasing Courage

Figuring out who you really are is scary because
1) you might have to change something, or
2) you're scared you might not have much
value to add to the world.

Your Values can guide your decisions and explain how you're feeling. When you're upset, your Values have been challenged. When you feel amazing, you're living true to your Values.

Your Life Purpose outlines the impact that you, personally, can have on the world.

Your Energizers are what you're naturally good at. Using your Drainers feels like work and it's exhausting.

A perfect life is living true to your Values, delivering on your Life Purpose, having lots of opportunities to use your Energizers while not needing to rely on your Drainers. And getting out of that comfort zone *often.*

PART 3 - TAKING ACTION

THE BUILDING BLOCKS

"A year from now you will wish you started today."
Karen Lamb

Holy crap we've covered a lot of big stuff. We've covered topics that many people *never* talk about. Most people will never ever figure out their Values, their Energizers and Drainers or their Life Purpose and they'll continue to be disappointed in life. Forever!

In order to get this far you've showed heaps of courage. Courage to figure out what matters to you and what you can be great at. You've addressed one of life's scariest questions: how can I add value so that I belong?

Let's revisit the chart we began this book with. Up until now we have focused on the vertical axis, getting "CLEAR." We are now clear on where fear comes from, the potential that courage has for our life, and we also looked at YOU specifically so you can better understand who *you* are, and we have an idea what your most satisfying Life Purpose might be.

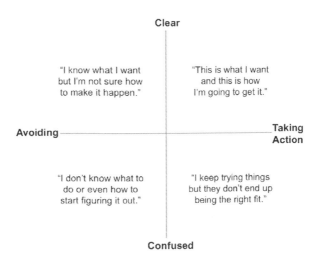

Clear

"I know what I want
but I'm not sure how
to make it happen."

"This is what I want
and this is how
I'm going to get it."

Avoiding ———————————————— Taking
Action

"I don't know what to
do or even how to
start figuring it out."

"I keep trying things
but they don't end up
being the right fit."

Confused

But if you thought we were just going to keep writing about stuff that you could absorb from your chair without ever having to get OUT of your chair, you were wrong! Now we'll be talking about ways that YOU can get out of that chair and DO SOMETHING ABOUT IT. This is where we jump head first onto the horizontal axis: Taking Action. You'll involve other people and you'll stop putting up with the things in your life that don't fit you.

It's a whole different ball game, though, when we start to engage other people. The Big & Nasty fear of "What will people think of me?" will be front and centre throughout. People may judge you. They may question what you're doing. They may think you're not "cool." They may think you're selfish for not being content with what you already have. That's scary.

And kind of exciting too.

The courage to not know

Story Time

That's me on the left before my first day of work after graduating university. I was working in marketing in London England. I felt invincible in my new suit with my fresh briefcase. I felt like a success. I finally felt like my Dad, the guy I have tremendous respect for! My life was going exactly as planned; I now had a desk job with a large, international company with a decent pay check and I was on my way to taking the advertising world by storm and running a huge advertising agency one day.

Almost 20 years later, that's me on the right. I'm a speaker, coach and author on the topic of "Finding the Courage to be You." Not a damn thing about advertising. I could never have predicted this path and I sure didn't plan to be as bald as an eagle.

The point is this: we cannot predict how things will turn out. That's a good thing. We always need to have goals and targets – something to aim at – but we have to understand they might change. Any company who makes a long-term plan and sticks to it to the letter, will go out of business. The same is true for you. Things change. YOU change.

Goals and guesswork both start with the same letter for a reason. Goals are educated guesses. As we continue through life, gathering more and more experiences and knowledge, our guesses get better.

When you make decisions in life - especially big ones - you will not know if they're going to work. This is true for everyone, including me. We never really know until afterwards.

So have a plan, but be open to it changing. Let go of the need to know everything all the time. Embrace the unknown – that's where creativity happens. Have the guts to change and adapt because nothing in nature survives without doing that. Change is scary, but so are regrets.

You gotta *do* stuff

Not everything will go as planned. Not everything *can* go as planned when you're living courageously and getting the most out of life. There are too many unknowns. So let's talk about a healthy mindset which you will need to adopt in order to go easier on yourself and see the positive in everything that happens.

Most people are on auto-pilot the majority of their life. They do stuff. They wake up, have breakfast, go to school or work or whatever takes up their days. They do do do all day. Doing something again and again doesn't teach us anything, unless we choose to reflect on what happened and how it went. If I have a sugary cereal for breakfast (mmm, Honeycomb), I'll feel more lethargic that morning than I would if I had something healthy. But if I don't take a moment to think about what I did, what the result was, and whether I'm happy with it, I didn't learn anything from the experience.

The same is true for a job interview. You can go in with an idea in mind of what you want to say and ask, but if you don't take a moment *after* the interview to reflect on the experience (what went well, what didn't) and then decide how you will do it differently next time, you have completely wasted that learning opportunity and the chance to be better.

Imagine you went into that job interview with a well thought-out plan. After the interview you took half an hour to review what went well, what didn't go well, and then you made a plan for what you would do differently in your next job interview. Imagine you did this every time. Your learning would skyrocket and you would become the Michael Jordan of interviewing.

Experiment, Reflect, Evolve

Reaching your full courage potential means deciding to be a lifelong learner. You need to be a kind of mad scientist who is always testing out new ideas, seeing what happens, and then adapting accordingly the next time.

Every single thing you do can be considered an experiment. How you put together a presentation, what you say on a phone call, how you look for a new job, what you do for fun on the weekend. It took Benjamin Franklin about 10,000 attempts to figure out the light bulb but he didn't consider those to be failures. Each time it didn't give him the required result he said, "That's one less way it might work. I'm getting closer." A lot less pressure that way, right?

The beauty of the word "Experiment" is that it implies things might not go as planned! This gives us the freedom to make more mistakes on the road to learning. What a relief! I believe that nothing is a mistake as long as it seemed like the right thing to do at the time the decision was made, and you learn something from it in the end. The words experiment and experience look and sound similar for a reason.

After you experiment with new behaviors or new ways of being, you then move on to "Reflection." What went well? What could have gone better? What did you learn? With that reflection and learning comes your "Evolution."

> "The mind, once stretched by a new idea,
> never returns to its original dimensions."
> *Ralph Waldo Emerson*

Evolution is when you take your learning from the previous stage and decide how you want to adapt your approach next time. You keep doing what worked well. You take what didn't work well and decide how you want to try it differently next time. Over time you continue to improve your performance.

It makes sense, right? Then why do so many people not take this approach? As we discussed previously, we are programmed to avoid change and not do anything that others might criticize us for. If we reflect on something and realize it's not right, it means we need to change something. With change comes unknowns and our fears of failure (and the negative opinions of others). As a result there is an absolute DROUGHT of reflection - and therefore awareness - that exists in the world.

Want to start tonight? Every night when my one-and-only and I go to bed we ask each other, "What did you like about today?" "What did you not like about today? "What did you learn from it?" "What are you looking forward to tomorrow?" You can do this too. It will help keep you from becoming one of the many human zombies that trudge through life and are surprised when they get old and things haven't turned out the way they thought they would.

Stop shoulding yourself

Some days you feel like a rock star and you kick bum all day. Other days you may feel like you're a boring character tagging along in someone else's fun story. The truth is, the words that come out of your mouth have a huge impact on how you feel. Every day we can say things that will empower us or we can choose slightly different words which will actually *disempower* us and make us feel like we're not in control of the situation and our life. The first option feels good. The second option feels poopy.

When was the last time you said something like this:
- "I'd love to do that, but I need to get some work done."
- "I want to quit my job and try something new, but I should probably stick to what I know."
- "I should go to the gym today."
- "I have to do the laundry."

There are some EVIL words in there that we should not use (crap, I just used one!): need / can't / have to / should. Those words make us feel like we're not in control when, in reality, we always are.

For example, we say "need" (or "have to") all the time but in reality you don't NEED to do anything. You don't even need to eat ever again. You'll die of course, but it's still your choice – you don't *need* to do it. You *choose* to do it.

And what about "should"? The truth is we should-all-over-ourselves all the time! "I should do this, I should do that, I shouldn't do this." Maybe you feel you should have taken a different job, should not have stayed up so late last night, should have said something in that important discussion, should have approached that hottie at the bar....

Don't be one of those pathetic people that have an excuse for everything in their life. You are in control of what happens in your life every single day. Nobody else is. Only you.

Everything is your Choice

As soon as you start seeing everything in life as your *choice*, you have grabbed your life by the you-know-whats and said "You report to ME now." You may still do things you're not too excited about, but the fact is you are consciously *choosing* to do them and therefore the ball stays in your court. You don't HAVE TO go to your in-laws for dinner because your spouse MADE you go. That's a total cop-out. You don't HAVE TO go to work on Monday, you CHOOSE to go. You could literally stay at home and watch TV all week and never go to work. You'll probably get fired, but it's still your choice where your butt sits. Your legs are yours - no one else is walking them for you.

In fact, it is impossible to *not* choose. If you stay home tonight and do nothing, you chose that. You choose to be reading this right now. If you never pick up this book again you are choosing not to read it. Even doing nothing is a choice.

"You are where you are because you put you there." Go back and read that two more times. It's the truth. Blaming someone or something else for what you have disempowers you, the blamer. And you know what else? No one really believes you anyway when you blame something else. But your ego makes you do it.

Have you ever had a boss (or a parent) admit when they did something wrong instead of making a lame excuse? "You know what, that was my fault and I apologize. What can we do to ensure it doesn't happen again?" You instantly gain respect for that person. They're not a weak, disempowered excuse-maker.

Let's be realistic - some things are indeed out of your control. The weather, a car accident, something bad from your past. While this is true, the part that is still in your control is how you choose to *perceive* it from now on. And what you choose to do about it. I can't control my receding hairline but I can control how I think about it! (I save a fortune on haircuts and it's natural air-conditioning in the summer). I can't control the crappy weather today but I can choose to stay positive anyway. See what I mean?

Remember my car accident I told you about earlier in the book? I didn't choose for that guy to run out in front of my car while his fiancée watched, but I did choose to be driving on the highway on that night at that time. Afterwards, I chose to write a letter to his fiancée because I was worried about her. I chose to see what I could learn from that horrible experience. And I chose to get back on the road the next day.

So, while I couldn't control the original experience, I could change my relationship with that experience and find the most positive way forward.

True freedom in life comes from taking responsibility for every single thing you do, because you saw it as your choice. Not someone else's.

Remember the rebel you felt like in high school? Leaving your bedroom a mess, staying out late, getting into trouble…. Do you know why you did that? Because you wanted to feel *in control*. You wanted to make your own *choices*. Are you one of those people that are always 5 minutes late? If so, you're choosing not to be on time. After all, would you be late for your mother's funeral? Probably not. You would choose to be there on time. When you get invited to events on Facebook do you prefer not to reply, or to hit "maybe"? Yeah, you want to keep the ball in your court. Do you ever stop the microwave when there are just a few seconds left? You want to be in control - you don't want the microwave to make decisions for you. I'm not saying you're a control freak, I'm saying we ALL do this kind of stuff. We're human.

In fact, do you ever notice if someone tells you not to do something, a part of you instantly wants to do it? You're a kid at heart! As adults we're just able to act all prim and proper. Little kids say what's on their mind – adults do not. All that being "proper" starts to fester inside us until we want to burst.

Okay, let's be realistic

In your own mind, when you're making decisions and weighing options, do not use those words I mentioned: need, have to, should, can't. But am I saying to never ever use those words again with other people? Of course not. When your friend asks you to go to his birthday party but you decide not to go because you want to take it easy and save money, it probably wouldn't be wise to say, "Hey, thanks for the invite but I'm going to choose to stay home and watch TV instead. That's what I want to do."

You can keep using those ugly words because they are what people are accustomed to. The trick is to make sure that you personally attach a *want* to the statement in your own mind. In truth, we only "need to" or "should" do something because of a bigger want. For example:
- "I *need* to go to the gym tonight if I *want* to feel fit."
- "I *should* eat healthier because I *want* to lose weight."
- "I *can't* go to your bachelor party in Vegas because I *want* to pay off my debts."

It's not an easy change to make and you won't master it overnight. I still find myself using those nasty words sometimes, but I'll catch myself in the process and change it. "I have to get up early tomor… no, I *want* to get up early tomorrow." "I need to work late tonight… no, I *want* to work late tonight otherwise my clients will be disappointed and they may fire me."

So feel free to continue using those ugly words with other people, but be sure to add a "want" into the sentence. And when you're talking to yourself in your own head, strike those disempowering words from your vocabulary right now.

If you're ever having trouble figuring out what the want is, take a look at your values and goals to see where the want may be hiding.

Think about your taxes. Not too many things feel more like a need and less like a want. But if I don't do my taxes then my business will be shut down. Then I can't inspire and empower people. In other words, I *need* to do my taxes because I *want* to inspire and empower others as best I can. So, in the end, I *want* to do my taxes.

I can't believe I just said that.

Comparing yourself to others

"Always be a first-rate version of yourself and not a second-rate version of someone else."
Judy Garland

Story Time

I had just returned home to Canada after working and travelling around the world for a couple of years. I was 26 years old and I was working in advertising. I was 2-5 years older than everyone else who was at my seniority level. As soon as I realized this, my Inner Critic starting yapping in my ear "Why has it taken you longer to get to this point in your career? Are you not smart enough? Are you destined for middle management? Imagine what they're saying behind your back." I made a joke of this one day and the response from a colleague was, "But you've travelled all over the world. You ran with the bulls in Spain and you hiked in the Himalayas. I've been sitting at a desk since I graduated university!"

It is so, so easy to fall victim to the comparison game. I feel fit until I go to the gym where I'm surrounded by personal trainers who make me feel like Jell-O. I feel like a success in my career until my buddy pulls up in his flashy new car that I couldn't afford unless I robbed a bank.

When I lived in France for a year I had days where I thought I was making a ton of progress learning French. Then I'd meet someone who had been studying the language less than I had and they were BETTER than me. Drove me nuts! "Oh hell, I might as well just give up. I haven't learned *anything*. I SUCK at languages."

How do YOU compare yourself to others? Salary, looks,

---

house, car, free time… the list can go on and on. Comparing ourselves to others is totally natural but it sure as heck doesn't make life any better for us. "Keeping up with the Jones" is exhausting and it rarely gets us what we really want. I know people that are so obsessed with keeping up that they must be miserable on the inside all the time.

Enter the Big & Nasty: we compare ourselves to others because we want to look good. We sometimes feel that the better we look comparably, the more people will respect us and want us around. In other words, we'll belong. In order to compensate for this, our natural inclination is to find some other fault with that person, just to make us seem a little less inferior…

- "Wow, she's gorgeous…but she's got fat ankles."
- "Yeah sure, he makes tons of money but what kind of a dad is he? I bet he's never home."

We can't help it! We were born as judgers.

On one of my favorite TV shows, the gorgeous super-fit babe in the show was telling her female friend that she was pregnant. She was so excited to share the news, thinking her friend would be equally excited, but the friend's reply was, "Oh my god, you're going to get fat!" And you could see she was absolutely thrilled about it until she realized what she'd just said and then tried to cover it up.

Whenever I did poorly on a test or exam in school, I always felt better about it if other people did poorly too. "You bombed it as well? Oh good, it's not just me, it must have just been super hard."

"You gained 10 pounds over the holidays too? Phew, me too. I might as well keep eating."

Inspire, don't impress

As soon as I start comparing myself to someone else, I ask myself "What inspiration can I draw from this person?" But it's not easy. My shallow side wants to start criticizing them and figure out what I might be better at. It's terrible! But cut yourself - and me - some slack. We're all human beings and we're doing our best with what we've got to work with. It takes effort to stop comparing ourselves to others.

> "The only person you should compare yourself to
> is the person you were yesterday."
> *Unknown*

By all means surround yourself with people who are doing amazing things. It provides learning and inspiration. Every truly smart boss is happy to hire people who are smarter than they are. You may have heard the saying, "If you're the smartest person in the room, you're in the wrong room."

Don't judge a book by its cover

When people are in public they present their best side, but that doesn't mean everything is golden in their real life. I hope it is, but it's rarely the case. When you're at a friend's house on Saturday night with a few other couples, don't base your opinion of their relationship on that night alone. It's the weekend and they're out with friends - of course they're happy and laughing and getting along. The grass is always greener on the weekend.

I've found that very few great things in life happen without a lot of hard work. That perfect-seeming married couple might actually be miserable. If they are indeed as happy as they seem, then they're both putting in the effort to make it a reality. It's not just happening on its own.

What's the happy ending?

If you continue to work at being proud of who you choose to be and stop comparing yourself to others, you eventually become happy for other people's success. It takes time, and even though I've been working at it for years I still have days where I'm tired and cranky and I just want to insult people behind their back. The person who is able to be happy for your success and all the great things about your life, is someone who is confident and proud of who they are. Focus on that, and you'll compare yourself to others less often.

Let's redefine "ambition"

One of the great things about being a speaker and coach is I get to learn from my clients. They often teach ME a lesson. I was once helping a client with career advancement and he said to me, "You know what? Maybe I'm not the home-run hitter I thought I was. Maybe some days I just need to get on base."

The vast majority of people (me included) put so much pressure on themselves to hit home runs every single day, and we usually equate that kind of ambition with our job. We're pressured at work to reach targets and we're inundated in the media with high-achievers like Oprah and Bill Gates.

But ambition is about way more than just your career. I believe ambition applies to all your Values and your Life Purpose. Your career is included in those things, for sure, but there is so much more to you. If someone chooses not to take a promotion at work it doesn't necessarily mean they're not ambitious. Maybe they realize the promotion would include a lot of overtime and they're nervous about not having enough time for their family. In that case they're being super ambitious with their "Family" value, and less so about career advancement.

If I skip a day of work to go for a big hike, that's ambitious towards my health and peace of mind.

My older brother is someone who is ambitious about being himself and he seems to worry very little what other people think of him. He's an inspiration for me that way.

Be fanatically *ambitious* every single day, but do it for all your Values and your Life Purpose, not just your "job." Today with this book I'm just going to get on base (I'll only write for a couple hours) but I'm going to hit a home run with my marriage (no, not that kind of home run, get your mind out of the gutter) by cleaning the house and buying my one-and-only her favorite yummy snack from the coffee shop around the corner.

OVERALL PROCESS FOR BEING COURAGEOUS

I'm so excited to be writing this part of the book, and not just because there's two feet of snow outside and it's colder than the other side of the pillow and I'm cozy as hell in my house with the fireplace channel cranked up to full volume and incense burning to give me the illusion that I'm in a cabin in the woods.

That's my best run-on sentence ever.

This is where I give you a *process* for using courage to be more you. This is a generic process for courageous decision-making which you can then apply to any and all of those changes you want in your life. In subsequent chapters we will look at specific steps you can take to get the changes you want and be more courageously you, but we start here with the generic process which needs to be understood first as it applies to every decision you make.

There are two ways to be courageously you: reactive and proactive. If you're meeting with your boss and he mentions an opportunity at work that scares the heck out of you, you ~~need~~ want to be *reactive*. If you want to stop arguing so often with your mother over your life choices, you want to take *proactive* steps to make that change a reality.

Whether opportunities fall in your lap or you seek them out, this process will help you determine whether something is a worthy opportunity to be more courageously you, or just a silly chance to be an unsafe risk-taker. After all, are you going to take every single scary opportunity that comes your way? No, of course not. Remember that some scary things are good, like the fear of falling off a cliff or the fear of petting a wild bear, no matter how cute it looks. Those fears keep you not dead and they keep both your hands still attached to your arms.

(Unless of course you're my brother who used to think if he was attacked by a bear in the woods he could simply shove his fist down the bear's throat and choke it. I'm not an expert on bears, but I feel like that would end poorly for my brother and his ability to give high-fives)

Scary decisions often have to be made in a work atmosphere too. Sometimes standing up to your boss will be a CLM (Career Limiting Move) and you ~~should~~ want to avoid it. Other times it's a necessary step to doing your job properly and adding value, being your authentic self and standing up for what you believe in so you can sleep at night and be damn proud of who you are.

GET CLEAR

Step 1: What's the Opportunity?

Identify the opportunity in the situation. With this book, you've already identified the changes you'd like at this point in your life. You can see how those changes can better serve who you are (your Values and your Life Purpose). They represent an *opportunity* for you to be happier and more effective with your life and the person you want to be.

Sometimes we actively seek out change, taking time to analyze and make decisions. But other times, opportunities sneak up behind you, tap you on the shoulder, and slap you in the face. When this happens, it feels less like an opportunity and more like plain old fear.

Story Time

I had just graduated from university and I was working in marketing. When I first sat down at my desk one of the admin assistants said, "Here's a catalogue for office supplies. Order what you need for your office." I looked at the catalogue like it was written in Latin. I didn't know what I needed for my office, I had never worked in an office before! "Oh great!" said my Inner Critic, "the first task in your new job and you don't have a clue what to do. You might as well quit right now - she's going to think you're a moron. That degree you took in university just went down the toilet."

The feeling of panic was overwhelming and my brain completely stopped working. I had to decide whether to fake it and pretend to know what I was doing, or be honest and tell her I had no idea.

In moments like that, fear slaps you in the face. I didn't seek it out.

In this instance I was lucky that she was a very supportive person! I walked to her desk and the panic must have been written all over my face. She took one look at me and said, "You don't know what to do, do you?" I swear my chin started shaking as I replied, "No, I don't." She said, "Don't worry, nobody knows when they're new."

The opportunity which fear was trying to mask was the opportunity to learn something new, show some honesty and vulnerability, and therefore grow as an individual.

Since fear is an emotion, we will first notice it through a *feeling*. I feel it first in my chest. My heart literally beats faster, whether the fear is right in front of me or I'm simply *considering* doing something scary. I feel a general tension or tightness in my lower chest. This is my first sign that something scary has presented itself and is therefore an opportunity to grow my courage muscle and be the person I want to be. But the emotional part of my brain kicks in and my Inner Critic starts trying to convince me not to do it. "This is a bad idea, Billy, it's not going to work. You'll look like an idiot. What will people think of you? You're not smart enough to pull this off. Don't do it, dummy!"

Exercise
Where do YOU feel fear first, physically? Many of my clients feel it in their chest, and others feel it in their neck, shoulders or their throat. Where do YOU feel it?

If you're not sure where you feel it, imagine a scenario in your life that typically scares you or makes you anxious. Perhaps if you screw up something for your boss or if you feel your spouse might be about to break up with you. Imagine that moment and notice where in your body you feel the fear. It can usually be pinpointed to one or two places.

The deal I have with myself is this: if something causes my heart to beat faster and that familiar tension creeps into my chest, I ~~have to~~ want to consider doing it. Every single time. It's a chance for me to grow my courage and be my true self. Does that mean I will do it for sure? Not necessarily. Keep reading.

Identify the Opportunities

Once I notice I am afraid and it's time to decide how to react, I then get my rational brain to kick in and do a bit of analysis before my emotional brain blows it all out of proportion. First of all, remember that EVERY scary thing is an opportunity to grow your courage muscle. That alone is a legitimate reason to consider doing it. But there may be another opportunity involved, so we want to ask ourselves, "What's the opportunity here?" Below are some examples:

Challenge / Scary moment	Opportunity
Speak in front of a group	Improve courage long-term, become a more confident speaker, maybe impress the boss.
Address an issue with a friend	Improve courage long-term, improve your relationship, get something off your chest, see if you can help them with something.
Take up a new hobby	Improve courage long-term, learn new skills and meet new people.
Talk to the hottie across the room	Improve courage long-term, meet a new person and possibly a long-term snuggle buddy.

Identifying any and all opportunities will help you decide if this is a challenge worth accepting.

Step 2: How Does it fit you?

Even though all challenges represent some kind of opportunity, you want it to *fit* with what's important to you and what your goals are. Ask yourself these questions:

- How does this opportunity align with my Values and Life Purpose?
- Does it align with my goals?
- Or is this simply a chance to exercise my courage muscle, with no bigger fit?

If it doesn't fit you in some way, don't do it.

Step 3: Is it worth the risk?

What is the worst possible outcome? What are the odds of that happening? And if it DID happen, could you handle it?

This is probably the hardest part. Our Inner Critic will try to convince us that the fear will put us in our Panic Zone (the bad place) because it doesn't want us to risk anything. Failure feels terrible. But would failure in this instance simply be *uncomfortable* for a little while, or would it be *detrimental* to you and your goals?

Most of the time the worst realistic outcome isn't actually that terrible. I find that committing to taking action is often *way* scarier than the action itself. We build it up in our head. When has this happened to you? For me, it's common when I ~~need~~ want to have a difficult conversation with someone. No one likes difficult conversations where you might have to let the other person know you're not happy with what they did, or you think they did something wrong. You want the relationship to be strong in the long term, but the longer you wait the more you build it up in your head until you're convinced the world is going to end as soon as you open your mouth. But you go ahead and do it anyway. You're thrilled it's over. And you know what, they didn't take it as badly as you thought they would. Phew!

> "The scariest moment is always just before you start."
> *Stephen King*

Very often in my business there will be something on my things-to-do list that I put off. I cut and paste it in the calendar on my computer day after day, convincing myself it's not the "right" time yet. I build it up in my head to be worse than it is. Eventually I realize I'm succumbing to fear so I take care of it. Nine times out of ten it is way easier than I expected, and the RELIEF afterwards is huge. It's not until then that I realize how much it was bugging me.

> "I've got 99 problems but 86 of them are completely made-up scenarios in my head that I'm stressing about for absolutely no logical reason."
> *Unknown*

Beware of Assumptions

This is when you start making assumptions automatically. Actually, it's your Inner Critic who does it. It wants you to assume the worst so you can have an excuse to avoid fear. The dreaded "What if's" pop into your head. "What if this goes bad? What if I look silly?" Don't allow the What If's to hijack your brain.

How many times have What If's stopped you from doing something that could have been a great opportunity?

Do you need to increase your expertise?

Sometimes it is not possible to do an accurate Risk Assessment without learning more about what's at stake. But sometimes you will ~~need to~~ want to know more before you can decide what to do.

> "When you feel helpless, you're far more afraid than you would be if you knew the facts. If you're not sure what to be alarmed about, everything is alarming."
> *Chris Hadfield, An Astronaut's Guide to Life on Earth*

As Chris says, you'll be able to do a much better risk analysis when you have more facts. Remember that Confidence = Courage + Expertise. Get as much expertise as you can (know the facts) and the decision of whether or not to accept a particular courage opportunity will be easier to make. If I grabbed someone who had never skydived before and put them in a plane and strapped a parachute to their back, they'd probably be pretty terrified. But if they knew ahead of time they would be skydiving and they used that time to research the facts about it (how safe it actually is, how few deaths there are in the world vs the number of skydives) they would feel more willing to make the courageous jump out of the plane.

Could I handle the worse possible outcome?

If you decide you could *not* handle the worse-case outcome, that's okay, but make sure you ask yourself, "Is it just fear that's holding me back?" If it is, re-look at your decision.

In order to help limit fear and ego from clouding your risk perception, answer these questions:
- What assumptions am I making?
- What advice would I give someone else in this scenario?
- Afterwards, what will I wish I had done?

Now you can accurately answer whether or not you ~~should~~ want to go through with the challenge. You either go through with it or you don't.

TAKING ACTION

Step 4: Commit

1) <u>Decide Not to Do It</u>

If you decide you could not handle the worse possible outcome that could realistically happen, you may choose not to do it. Doing nothing is still a choice.

If you decide that you could NOT handle that worst possible outcome, perhaps it is just a bit too big for you *at this particular time*. Ask yourself if there is a smaller version of this challenge that you could start with in order to grow your courage muscle. Baby steps are important because they increase our confidence for bigger challenges. If an opportunity to present in front of 20 people terrifies you and you've assessed there's a decent chance you'll mess it up when you can't afford to, then perhaps look for a chance to present to 1 or 2 people. You can always work your way up to a larger crowd, or, choose a topic in which you are super confident.

If you and your boss decide you're not quite ready to run a meeting, perhaps you could simply lead one of the topics in the meeting. A topic you know well and feel comfortable with. A good boss will give you a bigger opportunity later.

If you want to ask someone out on a date but the thought of rejection makes you feel like you're going to projectile vomit, maybe just send them an email about something you know they're interested in. See how they react.

Once you've identified a potential baby step, go back to Step

1, "What's the Opportunity?". Lastly, if you still say no, ask yourself "What am I giving up by saying no?"

OR...

2) Decide to Do It

You ~~should~~ want to choose to commit to accepting a scary opportunity when it aligns with your goals and the person you want to be (Values and Life Purpose) and you can handle the realistic worse-case scenario. However, no matter how brave or not we feel we are, we all ~~need~~ want help and support from time to time when fear is involved. Have you ever committed to doing something scary, then found yourself wanting to back out later? Yeah, me too. *All the time.* Below are some tips and tricks to help you stay accountable to what you've decided to do.

How can you use your Energizers and not your Drainers

Since we perform best when we use our Energizers and not our Drainers, always consider these two questions in order to help ensure success:

- Which of my Energizers can I leverage?
- Will any of my Drainers - the things I'm not good at - be necessary for this? If so, how can I *compensate* with an Energizer?

Story Time

At one point in my Outward Bound career I had a few weeks off in the winter. I was bored and feeling kind of down. My values which were low at that point were Adventure, Fun, and Value to Others. So I came up with an idea. I decided to walk from my cottage to Toronto to raise money for Camp Ooch - a charity for kids with cancer. It would be a 200 km walk (124 miles). In the middle of winter. The temperature at that point was -5 Celsius (23 F) and there were a few feet of snow outside. I would have to spend the first night sleeping in the woods.

This excited the hell out of me. It aligned with a whole BUNCH of my values. While I would definitely not be happy if I failed at this, I could live with it (barely). So I became more of an expert. I drove the route I would take to see how it looked. I researched how far a person of average fitness (i.e. me) could walk in a day and how much weight I could carry. I went for a 4-hr walk with a loaded backpack to see how I felt afterwards.

Then I committed to doing it. I told everyone I knew and I asked for donations BEFORE the walk. That way there was no way I was going to chicken out and have to return all the donors' money. What would they think of me if I quit?!

That walk is still one of the proudest accomplishments of my entire life. It took me 5 days and I raised $16,000 for kids with cancer. I was in the newspapers and on TV, which helped spread awareness. People would honk and yell encouragement as I walked. Some would stop and give me donations for the charity. As a result, the walk ended up honoring my Community value too, even more than I could have imagined. In fact, it honored every single one of my 10 values. No wonder it's such a highlight of my life.

Tell people about it

Since being accepted and liked by others is so important to us, once we tell people about our plans there is less of a chance we will back out because *"They might think I'm a quitter or a chicken!"* As a result, the more people you tell, the better chance you'll follow through. So tell lots of people. When I decided to write this book (a terrifying endeavor, believe me) I posted it on my Facebook profile so THE WORLD knew about it.

It's even more impactful to tell people whom you really respect and like. You'll want even *less* to have them think you're a giver-upper.

When I had a big, scary project to complete in my previous careers and I knew I was procrastinating, I would go into my boss' office and say, "You know that project I'm supposed to be doing? I'll get you an outline for it by next week."

Then I'm on the hook. I definitely don't want my boss to think I'm a procrastinator. Part of me is kicking myself for making the commitment, but I did it because it aligns with my bigger wants.

Imagine how it will feel after

Sometimes it helps to look forward to the outcome. How will it feel AFTER you've faced the fear? I often ask my clients "In order for you to feel amazing when you lie down in bed tonight, what do you ~~have to~~ want to do today?" Another great question is, "A week from now, what will you wish you had done?"

What's the first little step to get started?

Often the overall task seems totally overwhelming, but there is always a less scary way to start. If you're contemplating applying for a new job, step 1 could simply be to check out the company's website. For my big walk, the first step was to drive the route and see how it looked.

Set meeting dates with others

Often the biggest challenges we decide to undertake involve others. At work there may be colleagues or your boss that will be involved. In your personal life, if you're going to join a club maybe it includes a friend. In both cases, set dates with those other people involved. When you have it in your calendar with other people there is WAY less chance you'll chicken out.

For my big walk I contacted the charity I would be supporting and I asked for a written letter from them that I could send to people for donations, and I asked them to write the date of the walk on the letter. No backing out then.

Ask others who are doing it or have already done it

The best way to learn about something is to ask people who are already doing it. You could research for days online about a possible new career, or, you could have coffee with someone in that type of career who will distil years of knowledge into a half-hour discussion. The more people you talk to who are doing (or have done) what you're considering, the more real, hands-on learning you will get.

Ideally you can find someone who has been doing it for a long time as well as someone who isn't that far ahead of you. You'll get different insights from both.

If you've followed all those other steps, the doing part usually isn't nearly as bad as you expect it to be.

And of course, take care of all your baby needs; the three main things that make babies cry which NEVER stop affecting our mood no matter how old we get. Don't be tired, don't be hungry, and don't have to go to the bathroom.

Step 5: Evaluate and Evolve

And for gosh sakes, once you've tried the scary thing remember to reflect on how it went:

147

- What went well?
- What could have gone better?
- What would I do differently next time?

Now you have evolved and you're more prepared for next time when it will feel a tiny bit less scary.

A note about your Career

There are ample opportunities to be courageous at work: speaking up more in meetings, offering suggestions to your boss, asking for more challenges, standing up for what you believe in... the list is endless. However, there is sometimes more at stake with being courageous (and therefore possibly failing) at work than in your personal life. So how do we know what's a safe risk and what isn't?

Start with the process above and think hard about the potential impact of failure. If in doubt, ask your boss what they think. There is less risk of catastrophe if you have your boss' support, assuming you trust them not to throw you under the bus if the shit hits the fan. Connect your desire to do the scary thing with something that benefits your development AND the company's. For example, "Boss, I was wondering if you'd be comfortable with me running the meeting tomorrow. I've never done it before but I feel like I'm ready for it and I think it would be good for my progress. It may also allow me to take some work off your plate if you're okay with that. If so, I'd like your thoughts on how to prepare in order to ensure as best we can that I do a good job. These are my thoughts so far...."

Story Time

I used to be a fundraising director for a large international charity. For a while I loved my job because it was a perfect fit for who I was and what I was great at. My first priority was to improve the team relationships within my department across the country. I love that stuff. But once that was taken care of, I had to be a fundraiser which I suddenly realized I wasn't very good at and didn't really enjoy doing! As a result, it came as no real surprise when I got laid off during a massive restructuring.

So was it a mistake to take the job in the first place? Absolutely not. A decision is a choice we make with the information we have at hand. When I took the job it was exactly what I was looking for based on what I knew at that time about the company, the industry and myself.

By the time I was laid off I had way more self-awareness as well as industry knowledge. I now understood why it didn't work out, but taking the job was still the right move. Every job and romance I've ever had was right for me *at that time*.

By increasing our self-awareness we help ensure that we make better decisions in the future. Decisions that serve us as individuals.

Your Courage Card

This is a handy, short-form version of the courageous decision-making process. Feel free to take a picture of it with your phone for quick reference in the future.

GET CLEAR

Step 1: *What's the Opportunity?*

Step 2: *How does it fit me? (Values, Life Purpose, Goals)*

Step 3: *Is it worth the risk?*
- What is the worst possible outcome?
- What are the odds of that happening?
- Could I handle it?

TAKING ACTION

Step 4: *Commit*
1) Decide Not to Do It
- Is there a smaller version (baby step) of this challenge that I could start with?
- What will I be giving up if I don't do it?

OR...

2) Decide to Do It
- Which of my Energizers can I leverage?
- How might my Drainers get in the way?

Step 5: *Evaluate/Evolve*
- What went well?
- What could have gone better?
- What would I do differently next time?

Now let's take the courageous decision-making process and all that other stuff we've learned so far about courage and fear, and apply it to some of the most common ways that you will be challenged to be true to yourself on an ongoing basis:

- Who you choose to spend time with
- How you handle difficult conversations
- How you avoid - or accept - disappointing others
- How you can handle criticism and rejection without getting off-track

On Your Crew

"You are the average of the 5 people
you spend the most time with."
Jim Rohn

Your peeps. Your gang. Your crew.

They are the people you spend the most time with and feel closest to. Hopefully most, if not all, of those people in your Crew are adding more value to your life than they're taking away. But sometimes they're not.

Exercise

Make a list of the 5-10 people you spend the most time with outside of your working hours. For each of them, ask yourself these questions:

- Do they bring out the best in me?
- Can I count on them?
- Do they support me with my goals and dreams?
- Do I feel comfortable being 100% me when I'm with them?

With some people you let your guard down, relax and be yourself. With others you stand a little straighter, fuss about how you're holding your drink, or worry about how they'll react to what you're saying. That's exhausting and inauthentic. If I'm hosting a party I don't want to be thinking "What song should I put on that's hip and will make me look cool?" Instead, I want to think "F@&k yeah, baby, it's time for some ABBA!"

My mood is directly related to the people I'm with. So is

yours. Passionate, caring, *supportive* people make me want to kick ass and make the world better. Negative, gossipy, lazy people bring out the worst in me. We're like sponges, absorbing the moods of the people around us.

Don't get me wrong, I could sometimes win a gold medal in gossiping, but I try my darndest to notice it and stop it immediately because it's not the person I want to be. Some friends make that easier than others.

If the people in your life aren't making you and your life better, maybe it's time to kick them off your Crew.

After all, how many close friends do we *really* have time for? Social Media makes us think we *need* hundreds or thousands of friends and followers, otherwise we're a loser. If I have 2 or 3 really close friends plus my family then I consider myself extremely lucky. Who has time for more than that anyway? In the end, you only need 6 people to carry your coffin.

A study done by Matthew Brashears of Cornell University found that, on average, people had 2 close friends with whom they could discuss important matters. Some people had 0.

It's like the number of projects at work that you can do well: do you want to do an amazing job on 3 or 4 projects, or do you want to do a half-ass job on 10? Relationships are the same; they require attention and energy if they're going to be awesome.

You're (just) the captain

Imagine your life is a ship and you're the captain. You're the Big Cheese, the person in charge, but that ship ain't going anywhere without a Crew to ensure it's all running properly. Your life is the same. You make all the big decisions but without the right support structures and Crew, you won't get where you want to go. At the same time, a ship can have a Crew but if they're not the right fit (their goals, skills and values aren't aligned) the ship might still function but it's going to be a helluva rocky ride.

The Past is Powerful

It's one thing to meet someone for the first time, not really connect with them or see a fit with yourself, and therefore choose not to spend more time with them. But this can be much harder when it's someone you've known for a long time. Perhaps you became friends in high school or university and you've been buddies ever since. But 10+ years later you've both changed. Perhaps your values and interests aren't the same anymore.

Let me guess, it has something to do with fear?

You betcha! Of all the changes we may choose to make in our life, deciding to put less effort into friendships or let them go completely is one of the hardest. It plays on our deepest fears: our need to belong plus the Big & Nasty ("What will they think of you?")

Belonging
By changing our Crew we are giving up a relationship (i.e. belonging) that is established and feels safe. Looking for new Crew members means we may be turned down. We'll have to prove our value all over again in order to be accepted.

Big & Nasty
What will my Crew think if I make less effort to spend time with them? There's a chance they won't think too highly of me. Will they assume that I suddenly feel like I'm better than

they are? Will they think I've become a snob? Will they become petty and two-faced, talking negatively about me to other people behind my back?

Either way there's a chance they'll be hurt, and it never feels good to hurt someone's feelings.

It's about Values. Again.

Sometimes it's a case of your Crew being *bad* or a totally negative influence on your life. Those are simpler decisions to make. For example, if my friend calls me a loser and punches me in the face every time I see him, that's a pretty easy tie to sever.

But usually it's more a matter of values not being aligned. This sometimes happens when people have children. Their biggest value becomes their kids and sometimes (not always) they put less importance on other values. While I think this is the right thing to do because nothing is more important than being a good parent, if you yourself don't have kids then you and your friend's values might be less aligned than they were previously.

The same goes for partying. In university, it was a value I could have tattooed on my back. But as I got older my values changed. I still like to get silly and whoop it up from time to time, but it doesn't serve the values that are clearer to me now. Some of my friends are still in party mode and that's totally fine for them, but it doesn't align with who I am anymore.

Not having the same values doesn't make you right and them wrong and it doesn't make anyone better than anyone else. It just means the fit isn't there like it used to be.

The more values we share with our Crew, the more we'll motivate each other, the more we'll have to talk about and the more we'll enjoy spending time together.

Passion Powers Us

Passionate people are inspiring. They energize us. They make *us* want to be more and do more. I don't care if you're passionate about something I have no interest in, you'll still inspire me to do more and be better.

My friend Deb loves to fish. LOVES it! Going fishing is borrrring to me. But I'm still happy talking to her about it because I see the passion in her and that energizes me. If someone isn't passionate about something, I'll get bored of him or her quickly. Unfortunately I find a lot of people are passionate about nothing. Sorry, let me rephrase that: a lot of people *haven't figured out yet* what they're passionate about.

Your Spouse

The person you choose to share your life with is your most important Crew member! They're your first mate. The rest of your Crew is still crucial, but if you're struggling with something you'll usually trust your first mate the most. You had better, because you spend the most time with them and it's a lot of work to replace them.

Some days you will switch roles and they'll be the captain! My one-and-only and I call ourselves Batman and Robin. On some Valentine's Day cards I'll sign my name as Batman and other years I'll sign it as Robin.

With this most important member of your Crew, you ~~need~~ want some serious alignment, sharing some of the same

---

values. It's even better if your Life Purpose is similar, even if worded differently. My one-and-only and I have different Life Purposes but they are similar in terms of their impact on others. We call ourselves "Team Awesome." In addition, we wrote out a single Life Purpose for us as a couple:

"Inspire others to make the world better"

I firmly believe that any couple who is considering marriage - and DEFINITELY if they're considering having kids - should do the values exercise and see how they compare. It stimulates crucial conversations that can help avoid serious issues in the future.

One of my clients wasn't happy in his relationship so he compared his girlfriend against his values to test the fit. He went through each value and asked himself, "Does she take away from this value, or does she add to it?" He realized she was taking away from them more than she was adding and she didn't support him in what was important to him. He broke up with her the next day. When he started dating a *new* girl he showed her his values on the first date to see if those things were important to her too. They were, and they're still together 3 years later.

Of course it's not just about ensuring they add value to YOUR life. If your values are aligned then you will be more motivated to support THEM in everything they do. I believe romantic relationships aren't about each person putting in 50%, I think you BOTH need to put in 100% if you want it to work.

In the end, it's up to you

So many people blame others for their situation. Remember what we said about choice - we always have one. If a friend or relative is treating you like crap, that means you're allowing them to do it. People treat you how you let them. Don't make excuses so you can avoid making a change or taking responsibility. We all do it because we're human, but let's try to do it less often, ok?

Example: Applying the courageous decision-making model to my own Crew

The Challenge: I was not feeling aligned with one of my Crew
The Decision: do I let them go?

GET CLEAR

Step 1: What's the opportunity?

- Feel more supported and cared for.
- Remove their negative influences and maybe improve my own bad habits.
- Stop neglecting my top Crew members because I spend too much time on the wrong people.
- Live true to my Values and Life Purpose.

The above could be accomplished by 1) making an effort to improve the relationship or 2) stop putting effort into the relationship.

#1 is #1 for a reason - it should *always* be attempted first. If a ship starts having engine trouble, the captain doesn't automatically say, "Alright, we're probably screwed, so let's grab our life jackets and start fighting the sharks." Another Crew member would probably say, "But, captain, maybe we can fix the problem." The next chapter on confrontation will give you tools on how to actually approach these people and structure the conversation.

Step 2: How does it fit me?

Compare the person/people against my values. Which values does he support? Which does he take away from?

- He was taking away from Respect (to myself), he wasn't adding value to me as a person (Value to Others), and I felt he wasn't being Honest with either of us.

Does he support me in my Life Purpose or does he judge me?

- I felt like he was always looking out for himself, not me.

How does he make me feel about myself when I'm with him?

- We had tons of Fun together (one of my top values), but I didn't always feel great after we hung out.

Step 3: Is it worth the risk?

What is the worst possible outcome? What are the odds of that happening? Could I handle it?

- He might get upset or, worse, angry.
- He's also friends with my other friends. What if he speaks badly of me?

Also...

What assumptions am I making?

- He likes our relationship just the way it is. He's not willing to change. He doesn't care.

What advice would I give someone else in this scenario?

- "Have the talk! You owe it to him, yourself and your friendship."

Afterwards, what will I wish I had done?

- I'll wish I'd had the talk, for sure. Wow, this question always adds a lot of clarity about what's the right thing to do.

That question about assumptions is *critical* here. I may assume the other person wants the relationship to remain as it is, while in reality he's thinking the exact same thing I am! Maybe he's been avoiding this talk too. I find that when we feel something isn't right in a relationship of any kind, the other person/people feel it too. They may not realize it until you bring it up, but in my experience they are rarely shocked.

It sometimes just takes a conversation to get the change you want. They simply might not have known what was important to you, or they may have no idea they're acting in the way you're describing. It's up to you to let them know that. It's the ownership you ~~have to~~ want to take in every relationship.

They may reply, "Really, that bugs you? And that's important to you? Wow, I'm sorry, I had no idea." Or "I actually do those things? Wow, that's not what I intended. I'll be more careful." Crew member saved.

I'll also be a better friend by bringing it up. Maybe I can add more value to his life through the discussion.

TAKING ACTION

Step 4: Commit

1) <u>Decide Not to Do It</u>: don't give up on him

This applies if I decide the two of us are a good enough fit in terms of values and I miss spending time with him. In this case, I'm also worried about him and I think he's a bit self-destructive. Maybe the talk will help us both.

Is there a smaller version (baby step) of this challenge that I could start with?
- I don't have to make the leave-him-or-keep-him decision on my own. It would add value to have a conversation

and get our feelings out on the table and give him (and me) a chance to change if we both wish.

What will I be giving up if I don't let him go?

- If I keep putting up with the bad stuff, I won't be staying true to my Values and Life Purpose. Also, I won't be giving him a chance to change if he wishes.

OR…

2) <u>Decide to Do It</u>: give up on him

If I felt I had already done everything I could but I just didn't think the fit is there, it would be time to move on. I could simply back off and make less of an effort, allowing both of us to see what it's like without the other person around. One or both of us would either realize the importance of the other person and make more of an effort, or we'd realize it's time to move on with no hard feelings (hopefully).

Note: Obviously this would be a bit more complicated with a romantic relationship. You can't just back off and see what happens because they have a right to be told immediately how you feel. I know COUNTLESS people who just let a romance fizzle because they don't have the guts to address it! Have you ever done it? Be honest. Breaking up is HARD - by far the most difficult experiences of my life. But man up (or woman up), and do the right thing.

I find lots of people don't bring up an issue in a romance because they want to figure it out first before discussing it (I'm guilty of this). That's often an excuse to avoid bringing it up. Oftentimes you both ~~need~~ want to discuss it together to really understand what's going on. Even if you're not sure about something, I find it always helps to talk about it.

Which of my Energizers can I leverage?

- For me in this scenario, it would especially be Curiosity and Honesty. "Hey bud, we haven't talked for months so obviously something is wrong. I've been frustrated with our relationship lately. Wanna talk about it? I'd love to hear your side of the story too."

How might my Drainers get in the way?
* Forgiveness and Humility are two of my Drainers, meaning I'm not good at them. They will make this trickier because I will have to forgive and I may have to admit that I was the one at fault. That doesn't come naturally for me.

In the end I chose to address the friendship in hopes of saving it rather than assuming it was too late and giving up.

Step 5: Evaluate and Evolve

What went well?
* He was totally receptive and he apologized. It was helpful to start by taking ownership - I admitted that I could have addressed this issue earlier.

What could have gone better?
* I wish I had brought it up earlier. I had convinced myself it wasn't worth it, but inside I knew I was just avoiding the conversation out of fear of confrontation.

What would I do differently next time?
* Bring it up earlier.

Exercise
Go back to that list of your closest Crew. Which Crew members do you want to focus on more? Which do you want to focus on less? How might it be valuable to address any of the gaps with them through a conversation?

"A friend is someone who gives you
total freedom to be yourself."
Jim Morrison

Family

There are a few members of our Crew who are a *little* trickier to simply "get rid of," no matter how bad we may want to: our family.

In a poll I conducted while writing this book, the group who most influenced people's life choices was their family (59% of those polled) followed by close friends. The answer was almost the same for another question too, "Whose expectations or opinions most hold you back from being 100% you?"

Mmmm, family. Sometimes we adore them and we're so thankful to have them. Other times they drive us NUTS and we can't be in the same room. I've seen people be completely rational and sensible one moment but then two seconds later their parent or child does that one thing that drives them up the wall, and they completely lose their mind.

So perhaps with our family it's less a question of "Do we ditch them or not?" and more about "How can I improve what we have?" The make-an-effort-to-improve-the-relationship approach applies even more to family.

Entire books are dedicated to improving family relationships, but needless to say the process is similar to any other member of your Crew in terms of how you handle it. The main difference is that our emotions are *extra* sensitive with family members. The next section on confrontation helps us better understand how to handle this.

For now, just remember that everything comes back to values. If a family member is driving you nuts, try to figure out which of THEIR values they might feel are not being honored. People act out when they feel hurt or disrespected.

On Confrontation

Confrontation: A hostile or argumentative meeting or situation between opposing parties

----

Story Time

During my 12 years of leading wilderness trips for Outward Bound, I had participants ranging from 12-year-olds to 64-year-olds. From students and artists to company presidents and former editors of Hollywood magazines. The most challenging groups - and therefore the ones with the biggest learning opportunities - were youth-at-risk boys.

We did 3-week long canoe trips in the Canadian wilderness, many hours from civilization. The boys were 15 and 16 years old. They were tough and most of them had a real chip on their shoulder about something. On top of that, there were bears, snakes and mosquitos as big as your left butt-cheek.

One morning I woke up one of the tents of boys and said, "Greg, you're on fire duty today. It's time to start collecting wood." Greg immediately replied in an angry tone, "Yo, shut-up, you bald-headed mother-f%&ker."

At that point, I handled the situation terribly. I threatened to throw a pail of water on him in his tent - not very respectful! Soon after, I realized my mistake so I had a talk with them that smoothed everything over and made our relationship stronger than before.

There is a simple process to follow to get a positive outcome when conflict and temper tantrums seem to be beating down your door with no chance of escape. It applies equally to the story above in the middle of the woods as it does in a boardroom when someone verbally attacks you, or at home when your spouse fails to take out the garbage YET AGAIN. These are perfect examples of negative emotions sneaking up and slapping you in the face, making them very hard to manage.

I recently conducted a study of organizations and their Professional Development needs. The most common change these organizations wanted to see in their people was for them to speak up more and have those difficult conversations that every job requires at some point. After all, what doesn't get spoken out gets acted out later. As long as a proper process is followed, smart people always want those touchy subjects to be addressed.

Before we dive into the actual process that you can start using immediately, let's understand what's going on from a big picture perspective because then the process will make more sense.

It's all about words

Don't don't don't jump to conclusions (i.e. assumptions). Often in confrontation with others we discover it's not as bad as we first thought once we talk it out. Often we simply haven't understood the other person's point of view accurately. Remember your fear filter, muddling up everything you hear in order to make you look good. It's very possible that YOU didn't explain yourself properly and you've therefore given them an inaccurate picture of how you feel.

Reactive Conflict

It is one thing to confront someone with a touchy topic, but it is infinitely more difficult to deal with it when it sneaks up on you, initiated by someone else. Then you're caught like a deer in the headlights without time to prepare. Someone cuts you off in your car, your friend gets angry at you for something they think you did and unjustly accuses you. If we allow our emotions to take over our brain in these scenarios then we will continually make poor choices, say hurtful things, and end up with regrets.

How often have you had a confrontation with someone and been so flustered in the moment that you couldn't think of anything to say? Then they walk away and you start thinking, "Oh man, I should have said THIS. That would have been perfect."

Take a Break

The stronger I feel that nasty feeling in my chest, the more my emotions are trying to hijack my brain because my values have been compromised. If the feeling is REALLY strong then I know no matter how hard I try it will be very difficult for me to deal with this situation properly right now. I may have to buy time. Often we only require a few seconds to slow our brains down and start to be more rational.

One of the most valuable things I ever heard on this topic came from a great speaker who said, "If you're really upset or angry at someone and the first thing that comes out of your mouth feels good to say, it's wrong. Every single time." The right thing to say will feel HORRIBLE because it entails showing vulnerability.

The stronger you feel the negative emotion, the wiser it will be to buy some time and step away from the conflict so your emotional brain can release. One response that I've used is, "I just need a minute to think about that so I can answer properly." It buys me time and it shows that I'm also considering their best interests (answering properly).

R-E-S-P-E-C-T

I have found that what is always at the root of a confrontation is that one or both parties involved feel they have been disrespected. The boys on my youth-at-risk canoe trip didn't want to work every day as hard as they were required to. Far from it. But as long as I showed them respect, they were willing to cooperate. The second I was disrespectful, all hell broke loose and the trip ground to a halt. So how do you show respect at all times? You show you care about their needs and you practice vulnerability.

Sounds pretty lame, doesn't it? And not very fun either. But it works.

Unfortunately we associate vulnerability with weakness and that's why bosses, parents, teachers and loved ones often don't want to show it. Maybe it will make us look soft, at the whim of our feelings and emotions. The truth is, it is the most powerful tool for developing trust, stronger relationships, and resolving conflict of all kinds.

"Don't change so people will like you.
Be yourself and the right people will love the real you.
Unless you're an asshole. Then you should change."
Unknown

Example: Applying the courageous decision-making model to Confrontation

The Challenge: my camper was disrespectful to me and I felt angry, frustrated and disrespected so I lashed out at him verbally.

The Decision: would it be better to address the issue or simply let it go? If I address it, what's the most effective way to do so?

GET CLEAR

Step 1: What's the Opportunity?

- To show fairness and therefore increase the respect we have for each other.
- To diffuse something which could grow exponentially if left unchecked.
- To make our relationship stronger.
- To work more effectively together.

And obviously it would be nice to lose that horrible feeling inside that makes me want to break something or cry or both.

Step 2: How does it fit me?

Which of my values were stepped on?
- Community, Honesty/Respect, Value to Others. Note: it wasn't just him stepping on these Values when he called me a mo-fo, I also stepped on them when I didn't respond to him nicely.

Which of my Values could I honor by addressing the issue?
- All of the above!

What fulfills my Life Purpose better - dealing with this or leaving it alone?
- For sure dealing with it.

168

Do I value the relationship with this person?
- Yes. He's my responsibility on this course and he's a good kid, he's just had a tough upbringing and he's doing the best he can.

Is this relationship a necessity?
- For the remainder of this trip, yes.

Step 3: Is it worth the risk?

What is the worst possible outcome? What are the odds of that happening? Could I handle it?
- Will I make it worse by addressing it? Will he think I'm a complainer? Will I get emotional? Will he think I'm weak and try to push me more later? Will he get worse and be more of a pain in the ass?

Also…

What assumptions am I making?
- He's mad at me, he thinks I'm unfair.

What advice would I give someone else in this scenario?
- Deal with it ASAP! You know it's the right thing to do.

Afterwards, what will I wish I had done?
- I'll wish I had addressed it in a mature, respectful, professional way.

TAKING ACTION

Step 4: Commit

1) <u>Decide Not to Do It</u>: ignore the tension and don't address it.

Perhaps I felt like this has been an ongoing issue and I'd already done everything I could to resolve it.

Is there a smaller version (baby step) of this challenge that I could start with?

- I could ask my co-instructors if they have experience with this kind of thing. How have they dealt with it?
- I could instead focus on the GOOD things Greg does over the next few days in hopes that he'll appreciate the recognition and start to behave better. This technique is often very effective, especially with people who aren't used to being praised.

What will I be giving up if I don't do it?

- My integrity. Respect for him. I'd feel lazy and I'd feel like I wasn't providing him the value and effort that my organization (and I) strives for.

OR...

2) <u>Decide to do it:</u> address the tension

I decided to have the conversation because it was clearly better for everyone. I knew that my Inner Critic was blowing it out of proportion in my mind and it probably wouldn't be as bad as I was imagining. It's all about having a process that works, which we'll cover in the next section.

Which of my Energizers can I leverage?

- I could use Honesty (sharing my thoughts) and Curiosity (maybe I don't know the whole story - what can I learn?).

How might my Drainers get in the way?

- Forgiveness and Humility are hard for me and they'll both be needed. Self-regulation is also tough for me and it might cause me to put it off or lose my cool again.

Step 5: Evaluate/Evolve

What went well?

- The whole conversation! We both felt better after.

What could have gone better?

- I could have recognized earlier the tightness in my chest and maybe avoided my initial, disrespectful reaction.

What would I do differently next time?

- Try to catch myself before my outburst occurs.

V.O.M.P. - Verbalize, Ownership, eMpathize, Plan

If you get to the end of the decision-making process and decide to move forward to confront the issue, here is a simple process to follow. While not every single confrontation in life ends positively, this process provides the best chance of success. If you follow this completely, you will have done everything in your control and you can feel damn proud of yourself. But beware - you'll need to be vulnerable.

Models are always more easily understood if we apply them to a real-life scenario, so we'll use the previous example of the camper who didn't want to collect firewood and called me a bald-headed mo-fo.

STEP 1: *V*erbalize your point of view or goal

State your case as your opinion, not a fact.
Starting with "I feel like" or "In my opinion" shows that it's not a fact, it's just how you see it. That shows respect. It's even better to say, "I could be totally wrong here, but I feel like...." That's hard to say because it takes vulnerability; you're admitting that you may not be right.

Make the issue about you, not them.
As soon as you accuse someone of something, they tend to get defensive. They often close down and stop listening. You will get a much more open listener if you make the issue about you, not them.

About them (accusatory)	About you
"You didn't listen to me."	"I could be wrong, but I feel like you didn't get what I was trying to say."
"Why didn't you do the dishes?"	"I could be wrong but I thought we agreed you were going to do the dishes today."

Make the benefit about both of you
"I feel like we'll both feel better if we can sort this out." Or, "If we can figure out a better way to do this, I believe it will make both our jobs easier."

Always ask for their input
This shows the utmost respect because you're saying you value what they think. "How do you feel about this?" or "Do you see it differently?"

Our bald-headed mo-fo example

"Greg, I'm not okay with the way you talked to me back there. I found it disrespectful. I could be wrong here - and tell me if I am - but I think you knew you were responsible for starting the fire this morning. I want to figure this out so we're not pissed off at each other and we can avoid this happening again. What are your thoughts? And please tell me if you think I'm being unfair."

I absolutely love that ending and I use it consistently - "Please tell me if you think I'm being unfair." It shows so much respect for the other person. It's shocking how many people always assume they're the one who's right. I'm wrong all the time! I hate it, but it happens! People always want to look good, so being wrong doesn't feel good to our caveman programming and we therefore avoid it at all costs.

Sample Conversation Starters in a work context
- "I'm having this conversation with you because I value your input."
- "There's something I'd like to discuss with you that I think will help us work together more effectively. Do you have a minute?"
- "I'd like to talk about _____ with you, but first I'd like to get your point of view."
- "I would like your help with what just happened. Do you have a few minutes?"

- "I could be wrong but I think we have different perceptions about _____. I'd like to hear your thoughts on this."

STEP 2: Ownership

This is where we have to look vulnerability in the eye and say, "I'm not scared of you." I believe there's nothing more powerful than admitting to someone that you screwed up. It builds trust instantly. But most people avoid this because it makes them feel weak.

Examples
- "In hindsight, my email may not have been as clear as it could have been...."
- "I know I can get short-tempered sometimes when we discuss this topic, so I'm sorry if I didn't listen as well as I could have."

Story Time

Not long ago a guy cut me off on the road. I reacted by giving him the finger and yelling at him from inside my car. Not good! I followed him for a minute and realized, "Crap, that whole thing was my fault, not his." So I ignored every single aggressive emotion that my genetic make-up was feeding me, I pulled up beside him and motioned for him to roll down his window. He gave me a dirty look as he prepared for a verbal battle but I said, "That was MY fault." His jaw almost hit the dashboard and knocked over his smoothie. He said, "What a nice surprise!" Then he proceeded to apologize and try to convince me that the whole thing was actually HIS fault. He looked like he wanted to hug me. I think he would have added me to his will if I had stuck around.

Admitting you're wrong or at fault doesn't feel good. Ever. When I admit I'm wrong my face gets hot and I feel like there's a brick in my stomach. How does it feel for you?

Ownership seems especially difficult for many men because we often think we have to be tough and macho. I've also seen it be very difficult for some women in corporate jobs because they are afraid of appearing soft or overly emotional in a world where toughness is sometimes valued more than honesty and vulnerability.

If you want to live an extraordinary life then you ~~have to~~ want to be prepared to be wrong sometimes, otherwise you will not put yourself out there for new experiences and challenges, because you're too stressed about the outcome. If you haven't admitted to being wrong in ANYTHING lately, you're either lying to yourself or not living to your true potential. And your relationships will suffer.

Don't ever lie

If you have racked your brain about what might have been your fault and you honestly can't think of anything, you can say so. But there is a respectful way to do it, by giving them a chance to disagree:
"To be honest I don't feel like I did anything wrong here, but if you disagree then please tell me because I want both of us to feel good about this."

STEP 3: eMpathize

Show that you understand their point of view; how it looks from their shoes and the challenges involved.

Example
- "I can see how this would be frustrating because it has

happened before where someone didn't keep you informed."

- "If someone talked to me like that I would be upset too."

Note: never say "I understand" – it sounds patronizing. *Show* that you understand, as above.

Our bald-headed mo-fo example

"I don't blame you for wanting to stay in bed. The weather is crap out here and we had an exhausting day yesterday."

STEP 4: *Plan*

Make a plan, together, for how you can both avoid this in the future. Be sure to ask first for their thoughts and input.

Our bald-headed mo-fo example

"Let's figure out how to make this easier next time, ok? I'm here to help."

Not all of those steps are needed in every scenario, but it's valuable to go through all of them first - in your head or on paper - to ensure you've considered all options. I believe the most important parts are to take Ownership and Empathize with the other person's scenario.

Hey parents! This is also a fantastic process to follow with kids who aren't behaving. They want to know you understand their point of view before you move towards a solution. The trade-off is usually time; it takes time to go through this discussion properly. Sometimes you don't have that time and it's simply "Get in the car, you're not having ice cream today." Other times you have more time and you're not exhausted so you go through all the steps above so they *understand* your reasoning. If you want to learn more about how you can use these tools to improve the relationship with your kids, the best book I've read on this topic is "Connected Parenting" by Jennifer Kolari. Check it out.

Is there not a quicker method?

I know, I know, the above steps may seem like a lot of work until you get more practice and it comes naturally. Some people feel they should just be able to say exactly what's on their mind. Sometimes you can but it really depends on the relationship in question. If there is a ton of trust and respect already established, you can skip some of those steps and get right to the point. But the above process is a safer bet for getting the results you want.

Come on, give us something easier

Alright, alright, I'll give you a simpler model for when you're short on time, or worked up emotionally and can't think straight in the moment. It's not as good as the VOMP model but it's still WAY better than most people do. It's called the "Shit Sandwich."

- The top piece of bread: something positive about the other person
- The shit in the middle: the negative/constructive thing you ~~have to~~ want to say
- The bottom piece of bread: something else positive

Our bald-headed mo-fo example

- Bread: "Greg, I've always enjoyed your honesty and sense of humor on this trip."
- Shit: "But this is going to be a long and painful three weeks if you don't start taking responsibility for your jobs every day."
- Bread: "If you can get better at that, you'll be a really strong member of this group."

On Disappointing People

*If you never disappoint others, you are choosing
to disappoint yourself.*

How many of your actions and conversations are based on trying to avoid disappointing others? When someone asks you to do something you don't want to do, how would your reaction change if you knew they wouldn't be disappointed? Or, if they were going to be disappointed, what if you knew they wouldn't hold it against you (the Big & Nasty)?

Chances are you'd say and do what you really feel, more often. I know I would. I hate disappointing people. It makes me feel like a bad person. And it always will because we are programmed to please other people since it helps us to belong, right? We are people-pleasers by nature.

One place this shows up is in a job offer. When you're discussing what your salary will be, the golden rule is this: never be the first to offer a number. If you're being interviewed, you want the employer to offer the first salary number. If you're the employer, you want the person being interviewed to say the first number. Why? Because we don't want to disappoint or insult the other person so the boss will often quote a number at the higher end of the salary range, while the person being interviewed will say a number at the lower end of their salary expectation. We want to please!

Exercise

Go back to those changes you'd like to see in your life. How might those be different if you never had to worry about disappointing other people?

Disappointing others is simply an off-shoot of confrontation. While straight-out conflict makes many people think about how to deal with someone who might be *angry*, disappointment feels more like dealing with someone who is *upset*.

Neither is nice but I personally find it harder to disappoint people than to make them angry. Anger is often the other person's issues getting in the way but disappointment hits something deeper. It starts when we're kids. All we want is for our parents to be proud of us. As a teenager I would feel way worse if I did something that truly disappointed my parents, rather than something that just made them angry.

For grades 7-9, I went to one of the most prestigious private schools in Canada. When my depression hit me in grade 9 I didn't think I could take the academic pressure anymore while dealing with my depression. I switched to my local high school where I had a lot more friends and the curriculum was less focused on academics. It wasn't until years later that I realized a part of me felt like I had disappointed my parents. They never gave me any indication that I had done so, but my natural desire to please them was making me feel that way. Sorry, I mean I was LETTING it make me feel that way.

As I got older and continued to figure out better who I really was and what I wanted to do with my life, I was moving away from the kind of career that my Dad had chosen. He was a very successful corporate guy, and I wanted to be just like him. But I eventually realized the corporate world wasn't the right fit for me. I was having a really difficult time moving away from it and I finally figured out that it was my inner kid wanting to please my Dad. That Inner Critic was part of my filter and it was influencing the decisions I was making. Once I realized this I reminded myself that my Dad didn't care if I followed in his corporate footsteps, he just wanted me to be happy. He's one of my biggest heroes and the best Dad I could ask for - I was just putting all that unnecessary pressure on myself without realizing it.

Taking Ownership

Disappointment is based on one thing: expectations. When reality doesn't meet our expectations we're disappointed. So when it comes to disappointing others, we ~~have to~~ want to ask ourselves if we are partly responsible by giving false expectations. If I say yes to more than one social event on the same night I will inevitably disappoint someone because I can only be in one place at one time.

You don't have time to care about everything

I get annoyed by those fundraising people who stand on the sidewalk and try to get you to donate to their charity as you walk by. They're quite clever and sociable so they try to rope you in with something complimentary like, "Hey, cool coat! Got a minute to chat?" or "You look like you're having a great day - can I ask you a question?"

I always feel a tiny bit guilty turning down their invitation to talk. But why should I? They're strangers and they're harassing ME as I walk down the street. They don't care about me, they just want my money, but I STILL feel guilty! I have a new response, though. I say, "I already give to a different charity." Their inevitable reply is, "But you can always give more" to which I respond, "Yes I can, but I choose not to! Have a nice day."

The fact is we don't have the time (or money) to care about everything. There are 24 hours in a day, some of which you'll spend horizontal with a pillow. With a limited amount of time and money every day, we ~~have to~~ want to choose our battles. We will be happiest and most effective if we focus on what we care most about and what excites us.

Will I ever volunteer at a fundraiser to save the whales? Nope. I think it's a very important cause but it simply doesn't interest me. I will be way more effective with the things that excite me while aligning with my values. Those are my priorities.

Do you devote your days to fixing the problem of disappearing honeybees? No? Why not? Scientists predict that bees are disappearing and, if they do, over 100 kinds of food that we eat every day will cease to exist. Some say we will disappear as a species if we don't fix the bee problem.

So is that a worthy cause? You bet your ass it is! It's our survival. Will I do anything about it this week or next? Nope. It doesn't energize me. You could argue it "should," but the fact is, it doesn't. What motivates me and maximizes my skills is helping people have the courage to be themselves. So I focus on that. Maybe one of my clients will decide to save the bees.

Your Inbox

We have become slaves to our Inbox. How many times a day do you check your email or text messages? Here's a new way to look at it: your Inbox is a gathering place for other people's agenda. If you spend all day dealing with your inbox and voicemail, you won't have time to do what YOU are great at. If you don't disappoint others sometimes, you will disappoint yourself.

How to say NO

Often, disappointing someone simply entails saying no. When I turn something down, I will always follow it up with something positive like "Best of luck with that" or "Have a great time" or "I hope it goes well," because I sincerely want people to be happy and fulfilled. Saying no is SO crucial to you having the time and energy to focus on what truly matters to you.

Don't lie

No matter what, always be honest. Never make up an excuse when you're saying no. You'll get found out. That's the annoying thing about lies, they always seem to come back to haunt us. In the brilliant words of Mark Twain: "If you always tell the truth, you never have to remember anything."

Always tell the truth, respectfully.

Keep it short

Whatever you do, don't give a long-winded explanation why you're saying no - it sounds less believable. If you aren't going to attend an event, for example, don't give a full explanation about how your dog is sick and you really *should* fix the leak under the sink blah blah blah. You know those long emails with every excuse in the world?

Keep it short and to the point. It always seems more believable when I hear someone simply say, "Thanks very much but I've already got plans." You don't have to share those plans because they're irrelevant. If they respect you as a person and they trust you, they will get it.

Disappointing through poor delivery

For me, the toughest form of disappointment is when I don't deliver on what I said, or I deliver poorly. In that instance I try my best to do the following:

- I take ownership and admit that I could have done better. I offer a reason, not an excuse. An excuse gets you off the hook, a reason is simply why you didn't deliver. "The reason this is late is because I underestimated how much

time it would take."
- Offer a solution for next time. "Next time I'll set aside a bit more time."
- Offer a solution if your deliverable isn't good enough. "If you're not happy with this then let's figure out a way for me to improve it."

Overcommitting

Our discomfort with saying no leads to overcommitting. This has taken me YEARS to improve and I still screw it up sometimes. But I screw it up less often than I used to, so that is progress, and I'll keep working on it.

As always, you want to figure out WHY you tend to overcommit. How is the Big & Nasty involved? What are you trying to avoid? I sometimes overcommit when I'm trying to avoid something bigger and scarier. I committed like a madman to all sorts of stuff when I didn't want to write this book!

Here are some nice ways to say no:
- "I can't commit to this as I have other priorities right now."
- "I'm in the middle of something right now. How about we reconnect next week?"
- "Let me think about it and I'll get back to you tonight." This one's my favorite! It buys me time and allows me to figure out if I really want to say yes.

If you're 100% sure you're not interested in what's being offered, there is no problem with being totally honest: "Thanks for offering but it's not really my thing."

Example: Applying the courageous decision-making model to Disappointing Others

The Challenge: when we planned our wedding venue we weren't going to have enough space to invite everyone who expected to be invited.

The Decision: do I stick to my wishes and not invite them, thereby disappointing them?

GET CLEAR

Step 1: What's the Opportunity?

- To have the wedding we dreamed of.
- To give me the time and energy to focus on the relationships which are most important to me.
- To not feel stressed because I've overcommitted.

Step 2: How does it fit me?

How will my Values be affected if I choose to disappoint? If I choose not to? How does it relate to my Life Purpose?

- Either way this will impact my value of Community. It's also a chance to be really Honest and do it in a Respectful way.

Step 3: Is it worth the risk?

What is the worst possible outcome? What are the odds of that happening? Could I handle it?

- I may upset some people or put the relationships at risk. Would they or their spouses give up on me? Will they feel they put more effort into this relationship than I do and be upset about it?

Also…

What assumptions am I making?
- They won't understand if I tell them they can't come.
- They'll hate me for not inviting them and they'll talk bad about me to other people.

What advice would I give someone else in this scenario?
- "It's your wedding for f#$k sakes, do what feels right for YOU! If they don't respect that, then maybe they're not that great a friend after all."

Afterwards, what will I wish I had done?
- I'll wish I had focused on the people that were most important to me.

As I've made clear already, we will always feel better when we treat people well. That's the difference between disappointing them and insulting them. I contacted the people I thought would be disappointed if they weren't invited and I explained the situation: we had limited space given the venue we had chosen so I couldn't invite everyone. That was the truth.

TAKING ACTION

Step 4: Commit

1) <u>Decide Not to Do It</u>: choose not to disappoint them, and just invite them.
Is there a smaller version (baby step) of this challenge that I could start with?
- I could check with some friends whose opinions I trust and get their thoughts.

OR…

2) <u>Decide to Do it</u> - risk disappointing them by not inviting them.

I decided not to invite them. I was worried how it would play out but I first gave myself a little pat on the back for having the courage to do it. I considered the VOMP model (and Shit Sandwich) to figure out how to approach the discussion best.

Which of my Energizers did I leverage?
- I used Honesty, Curiosity (to consider their perspective), and Bravery to go through with it.

How might my Drainers get in the way?
- In this instance I didn't see them getting in the way. But that didn't mean it was easy to do.

Step 5: Evaluate / Evolve

What went well?
- I was proud that I took the time to explain it to them.

What could have gone better?
- Not everyone reacted in a way I thought was supportive, but that was out of my control.

What would I do differently next time?
- Next time? I hope there won't be a 'next time' I get married.

On Criticism & Rejection

"If you don't stand for something
you will fall for anything."
Malcolm X

No one likes being criticized. How would it feel if someone said any of these things to you:
- "That's a terrible idea."
- "I can't believe you're acting that way."
- "Wow, you are *not* very good at that, are you?"
- "Are you feeling sick? You look exhausted."

Criticism: the expression of disapproval of someone or something based on <u>perceived</u> faults or mistakes.

If you're going to live true to yourself and base your decisions less on other people's expectations or stereotypes, then you will ~~have to~~ want to be ready for criticism. There's no way around it. If you are NEVER being criticized in your life, there's a good chance it's because you're conforming. If you step out of your comfort zone, say what's on your mind, or stand up for what you believe in, criticism won't be far away.

When you stand for something - such as racial equality, for example - you automatically stand against the opposite (racism). And there are always people who stand for the thing you stand against. Show me someone who is liked by everyone and has never ruffled any feathers and I'll show you someone who stands for nothing.

As you continue to step out of your comfort zone you will eventually make mistakes and you may be criticized for it. It's inevitable! The most successful people see criticism as an opportunity to learn and improve.

Criticism on steroids

The ultimate form of criticism is outright rejection. It's the worst! How would it feel if someone said any of these things to you:

- "We don't think you're the right person for this."
- "I don't think this is working out."
- "Sorry, you're not invited."

And the absolute worst one of all: "We need to talk." Ahhhh! Those are the four worst words to hear. You just know it ain't going to be fun.

Rejection: a) the dismissing or refusing of a proposal, idea, etc.
b) the spurning of a person's affections.

When someone criticizes something you said or did, they're usually just criticizing the action, not you as a person. But rejection hits an even deeper nerve because it seems like it's not just about your actions but *your entire self.* That feels terrible because of the Big & Nasty (the fear of what others think of us) and our need to belong. If we get rejected, we're being abandoned and evolution tells us it means death. That's why the second definition above usually hits you way harder than the first.

As a result we often get defensive and we start rejecting the rejection! We try to protect ourselves from looking bad. The healthiest way to deal with criticism and rejection is to consider two things: fit and insecurities.

Fit

Remember, every healthy relationship in your life including your relationship with your job/company is based on fit. If someone doesn't like your idea or if they don't want you around, it's often just a matter of fit. I've seen people offer solutions in meetings that were creatively brilliant, but didn't apply to the problem at hand. They didn't fit.

Any time I've broken up with a girlfriend or been broken up with, I wasn't rejecting the person, I was rejecting how well our two personalities/wants/needs fit together. They were still good quality individuals, but someone else will be able to make them happier than I can. And vice versa.

Insecurities

If there is one thing the human population is not lacking in, it's insecurities. We all have them. Every client of mine, no matter what their challenge, is surprised to hear that other people share the exact same fears and insecurities they have. So how do insecurities relate to criticism and rejection?

Every single time we say something to someone, it is coming from a place of Love or Fear. You can listen to two people having a heated discussion and figure out what each of them is scared of without them actually saying it.

When we say something to someone we do it in a way that shows we care about that person and have their interests in mind, or we're showing our insecurities by trying to make our issues theirs. When you say something negative or insensitive to someone, it's your own issues getting in the way. If a guy cuts me off in the parking lot and I start yelling at him and calling him names, that's my own fear; my insecurities that people aren't showing me respect and maybe I don't deserve respect. Responding from a place of love would have me saying instead, "Hey, I *feel* like you cut me off back there and that kind of pissed me off, to be honest. Is everything ok with you?" I'm showing that I care about the other person.

Note: If the word "Love" seems a bit extreme for you, feel free to use the word "caring" instead. They mean the same, but lots of people get the heeby-jeebies around words like love and feelings and emotions. It offends their inner caveman and makes them feel like a softie. I used to be one of those people but with practice I'm getting more comfortable with it.

Love love love love love.

Non-constructive criticism is a result of low self-esteem. Any time someone criticizes without showing love, I remind myself that it's based on an insecurity of theirs and it's as much about them as it is about me. It doesn't get me off the hook - I may totally deserve the criticism - but it helps me keep my cool in the moment and not think the person is a complete prick.

When a colleague rolls her eyes at your comment in a meeting, that's *her* issue. She might be worrying that she's not smart enough to be there (this is very common for men and women). Maybe she feels she needs to prove herself because you have an MBA but she doesn't. Many times I've had clients whose education doesn't match the job they're presently in. Their Inner Critic tells them that everyone thinks they're a fake, so they try to compensate sometimes and it comes out as aggression.

> "Honesty, without compassion and understanding,
> is not honest, but subtle hostility."
> *Rose N. Franzblau*

When someone says something negative about the new - and slightly edgy - outfit you're wearing, that's their own insecurities. Maybe they don't have the guts to wear something like that, or maybe they're worried your outfit makes them look dull. Responding from a place of love might sound like this, "Wow, that's a really unique outfit you're wearing. It's not my style but I respect anyone who has the guts to express themselves like that. Where did you get it?"

Extremely often, criticism and rejection are based in this example of fear and insecurities. People feel smarter when they criticize because it implies they could have done better. When presented with an idea, we don't always feel like we're adding value if we say, "Yeah, that's a good idea." Criticizing sometimes makes us feel smarter because we feel like we've added something. At work, it takes self-confidence and courage to say, "You know what, that's really well done. I have nothing to add."

Let's compare a challenge addressed through Love vs Fear.

FEAR
• Your boss: "This report is crap. Did you leave it to the last minute?"
LOVE
• Your boss: "This report isn't exactly what I had in mind, but maybe I wasn't clear about what I was looking for. Let's try to figure out what went wrong. Does that make sense?"

FEAR
• Your spouse: "Are you going out again tonight or do you think you could maybe clean the house once this year?"
LOVE
• Your spouse: "I don't feel like you've been helping out as much lately. Normally you're pretty helpful, can we talk about this?"

There is ALWAYS a respectful, loving way to get your point across.

Love love love love love.

Example: Applying the courageous decision-making model to Criticism and Rejection at work

<u>The Challenge</u>: I was once criticized at work for using humor too much with clients.

<u>The Decision</u>: Do I accept it or ignore it? How could I turn this into a positive thing by responding (internally or externally) in a way that I can learn and avoid negatively judging myself, my self-worth, and seeing my humor as a weakness?

GET CLEAR

Step 1: What's the Opportunity?

- To learn better how I'm perceived by others.
- To ensure people understand who I really am.
- To be taken seriously in my career and considered a positive contributor, not just a clown.

Step 2: How does it fit me?

How does the comment relate to my Values and Life Purpose?

- The comment affected my ability to add "Value to Others." I clearly wasn't living true to that. I also wasn't showing as much Respect as I could. This negatively affected my Community at work.

Which Values can I honor by finding a positive outcome to this situation?
- All of the above.

Note: Sometimes you look at your Values and Life Purpose and realize, "Hmmm, I hear what he's saying, but I honestly don't think I was inappropriate. I think I was being the person I'm happy being. I'll think more about what he said but I think I'm going to continue as I was."

Step 3: Is it worth the risk?

What is the worst possible outcome? What are the odds of that happening? Could I handle it?

- People may get the wrong perception of me.
- If I don't address this it might bother me and hurt my confidence in the future. Avoiding criticism or rejection does not make it go away. It's like a moldy piece of bread you sweep under the rug - you try not to think about it, but it just gets worse until it stinks like hell and friends stop visiting.

The only real risk in addressing this kind of challenge is that I will have to admit that I made a mistake. So I remembered the O in VOMP which stands for Ownership, by asking myself, "How might what they said about me be true?" Perhaps I was doing it as a way to compensate for being new to the job and not being totally comfortable with it yet. Yep, I think that's what it was: my own insecurity.

Also...

What assumptions am I making?
- My behavior isn't fixable. People are mad at me. It's too late to change it.

What advice would I give someone else in this scenario?
- "Address it! Learn from it so you can improve."

Afterwards, what will I wish I had done?
- Addressed it! And be more cognizant in the future of when I'm using Humor and whether I'm doing it to compensate for my own insecurities.

TAKING ACTION

Step 4: Commit

1) <u>Decide Not to Do It</u>: ignore the criticism and carry on as is.

Is there a smaller version (baby step) of this challenge that I could start with?
* If I wasn't confident about how to change my behavior I could simply ask my boss for advice in order to help me figure out how to improve my behavior or clarify the misunderstanding.

What am I giving up if I don't do it?
* If I do nothing about this then I risk it happening again and not benefitting from the feedback in some way.

OR…

2) <u>Decide to Do It</u>: address it and try to improve

Which of my Energizers can I leverage?
* Honesty, Bravery, Judgment. Not 'Humor' this time!

How might my Drainers get in the way?
* Humility! That's hard for me to show, but I could compensate by using my Curiosity to see it as a learning opportunity.

What's the first little step?
* Admit to myself that it's worth trying.

Tell people about it
* I told my boss and mentioned that I may check in with her more often on this topic to ensure I'm making the right improvements.

Imagine how it will feel after
- Good! Knowing I'm better at my job and more respected by my team.

Set meeting dates with others
- I could add the topic to our monthly status meeting.

Ask others who are doing it / or have already done it
- I could ask my boss if she knows anyone else who has struggled with this.

In the end I chose to address it and improve.

Step 5: Evaluate/Evolve

What went well?
- I learned how to communicate better, I gained more respect from my boss for making the effort, and I was taken more seriously by my clients.

What could have gone better?
- Not much to be honest. I was proud of how I handled it and took ownership for my behavior.

What would I do differently next time?
- Not much! Yay me!

OVERALL CONCLUSIONS
"Your Comfort Zone is Killing You"

As a reminder - and for quick reference in the future - here are the main conclusions from the "Getting Clear" section earlier in the book. It's now easy to see how it all affects the Taking Action section we just covered. Feel free to put these conclusions under your pillow, tattoo them to your arm or staple them to your forehead. Or just go to this page every once and a while when you feel they could help you.

On Courage

- Courage is hard because it can't exist without fear.
- Courage only feels good afterwards.
- Courageous people are scared.
- Courage is being scared and doing it anyway (because of a bigger want).

On Fear

- Fear is normal. You're normal.
- Fear will always exist when you're being courageous.
- The number 1 fear that holds you back from being you (the Big & Nasty) is the fear of what others will think of you.
- Your Fear Filter gets in the way of how you see the world.
- Your Inner Critic tries to get you to take the safe, non-scary option even when the more courageous option could be great for you.

On Increasing Courage

- Courage is a muscle.
- You grow it by exposure: stepping out of your Comfort Zone in order to face fear.
- Courage is relative. If something scares you, it counts,

regardless of what anyone else thinks.
- Confidence = Courage + Expertise

On You

- Figuring out who you really are is scary because...
  - 1) you might ~~have to~~ want to change something, or
  - 2) you will ~~need to~~ want to address whether or not you add any value to the world.
- Your Values can guide your decisions and explain how you're feeling. When you're upset, your Values have been challenged. When you feel amazing, you're living true to your Values.
- Your Life Purpose outlines the impact that you, personally, can best have on the world.
- Your Energizers are what you're good at and what comes naturally. Your Drainers feel like hard work.
- A perfect life is living true to your Values, delivering on your Life Purpose, having lots of opportunities to use your Energizers while not needing to rely on your Drainers, and getting out of your comfort zone often.

NOW WHAT ?

Holy smokes you're almost done.

Hopefully at this point you don't feel like your head is going to explode. It might feel that way. We've covered some big stuff.

Now that you've finished this book you can come back to it whenever you feel stuck. I recommend skimming over it once a year to see what might have changed for you and whether you're still on track to being who you really want to be. You may notice your values have moved a bit, or the things on your unhappy list have been replaced by new things. The cycle never ends, we can just improve our ability to manage it all effectively.

Exercise

We started this book with the below graph. You were asked to put each of the items in your unhappy list into one of the 4 quadrants. Now that you've finished this book, where do they fit now?

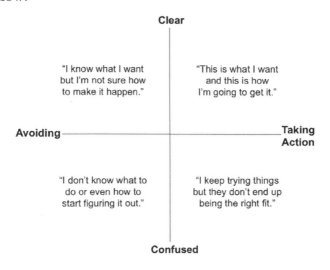

"You have brains in your head,
you have feet in your shoes.
You can steer yourself any direction you choose.
You're on your own and you know what you know,
and you are the guy who will decide where to go."

Dr. Seuss

Do this today

1. If you haven't yet, put your Values, Life Purpose, Energizers and Drainers somewhere you'll see them every day. As the screensaver on your phone, or a piece of paper beside your bed, or on your bathroom mirror. Read them once every day. Make them a part of your daily life, just like brushing your teeth. Let them guide you every day!

2. Pick the section(s) of the TAKING ACTION portion of this book that you feel could benefit your life the most. Your Crew, Disappointing Others… whichever would be most valuable for you. How can you start to put it into practice?

3. Sign up at **www.couragecrusade.com** to join the Crusade and get free access to my ongoing Courage Webinars plus other fun stuff.

4. Share this book with people you know who might benefit. Spread the love, folks!

5. Please please share your thoughts with us at **www.facebook.com/CourageCrusade** so I can continue to improve this book. What did you like? How did it affect your life? What are you doing differently now? How are you living true to yourself?! We'd love to hear your stories! You can also email me personally at sayhi@couragecrusade.com

I *never* get tired of hearing from my readers and followers. Never ever ☺

T.G.I.O.
(Thank God It's Over)

At the end of most books the author simply has a list of acknowledgements and that's it. Like it's no big deal. Are you kidding me?! I just wrote a BOOK.

Writing a book is hard. Very hard. It's a huge time commitment. There is a big chance you might never finish it or, worse, you publish it and nobody likes it! It's truly amazing how creative I was in coming up with excuses every day to not write this book. If I had taken that energy and creativity and applied it to actually writing the book, I could have finished it months earlier and stressed about it a lot less.

But I'm still pretty damn proud of myself, thank you very much. To write a book you need tons of self-regulation and perseverance, but since those are both Drainers of mine it meant that writing a book was going to be extremely difficult for me. And it was.

But that's enough about me, let's talk about you. What do *you* think of me?

That cracks me up every time. Just kidding, though, let's actually talk about you.

You just finished a book that can significantly improve your life if you do the work. Good for YOU. Lots of people say they want to improve their life, or change something, or be something different, but they never get around to doing it. I'm not impressed by what people *want* to do, I'm impressed by what people are *doing* right now. You just finished this book. I'm impressed you did and, more importantly, I hope you are too. After all, my opinion of you doesn't matter. Only your opinion of you matters.

Thank you, thank you, thank you for letting me be a part of your journey of growth. Let's pour ourselves a glass of our favorite drink right now, boozy or not, and toast each other for completing this journey together. We're both awesome.

Billy Anderson
Founder, The Courage Crusade

MY CREW

When I finish reading a book I would rather light my private parts on fire than read the acknowledgements. It's a list of a bunch of people I've never met and probably never will.

But this book would not have been possible without the help I received from a whole bunch of people. This page is for them. Calling them my "Acknowledgements" doesn't do them justice though. They are truly my amazing Crew.

My one-and-only Joelle

Mama Bear and Papa Bear

Mikey, Jon-boy, Virg

Super-intern Flo

My buds Deb, Whitey and CK

My inspiration to be better: Orrin, Ayanna and Eric Bishnooz

My star-studded sounding board: Corrie, Holly, Alexandra, Sloozy, Jackie

Juicy Brucey

About The Author

Billy Anderson - Founder, The Courage Crusade

When Billy was 5 years old his mom heard him crying in his room. She came in to see what was wrong and Billy said, "You're born, you live for a while, and then you die. What's the point?"

Now Billy helps other people figure out their "point" by finding the courage to be themselves. Billy leads by example. He had the guts to stop doing what the world told him he *should* do. Instead, he figured out what he *wanted* to do and the type of person he wanted to be.

That entailed escaping from his comfort zone on a regular basis. He has traveled to over 30 countries. He has jumped out of an airplane exactly 101 times. He has trekked in the Himalayas, run with the bulls in Spain, and swam with sharks in Asia and South America. He has been a sugar-cane farmer in Costa Rica, an apple picker in New Zealand, as well as an Outward Bound instructor, advertising manager and non-profit executive in Canada.

To join the crusade or to book Billy for a speaking gig, go to **www.couragecrusade.com**

the courage crusade.
Find the courage to be you.

Made in the USA
Charleston, SC
22 October 2014